SPELLING: GRADE
Table of Contents

Introduction ....
Record Sheet ....
Letter to Parents 4
Unit I. Social Studies
    Industrial Revolution 5
    Geography 8
    Election/Government 11
    Ancient Times 14
    Coming to America 17
    Mexico 20
Unit II. Art
    Impressionism (Monet & Van Gogh) 23
    Architecture (Frank Lloyd Wright) 26
Unit III. P.E.
    Health 29
    Sports 32
Unit IV. Music
    Music & Dance of Mexico 35
    Terms 38
Unit V. Science
    Laboratory Equipment 41
    Human Body 44
    Technology 47
    Chemistry 50
    Heredity 53
    Astronomy 56
Unit VI. Language Arts
    Gary Paulsen/*Hatchet* 59
    Paragraphs 62
    Kinds of Literature 65
    Research Paper 68
    Journal Writing 71
    Media 74
Unit VII. Math
    Probability/Statistics 77
    Graphs 80
    Pre-Algebra 83
    Geometry 86
    Money 89
    Tools/Terms 92

Answer Key 95
Assessment 97
Spelling Demons 97

SPELLING
A Thematic Approach
in content areas Grade 6

The National Council of Teachers of English has been conducting a study on spelling in the elementary school. One area of focus includes, "Is spelling taught or caught?" Is spelling learned through memorization of a sequence of letters? Or, is it learned through practice in language-rich reading and writing programs? We offer this spelling program as a thematic approach with word study skills included in each lesson.

ORGANIZATION

The book is organized into seven units, with two to six lessons in each unit. The units include social studies, art, p.e., music, science, language arts, and math. The three-page lessons are based on typical content presented in sixth grade. Activities in each lesson include word study for application of sound/letter patterns, research, writing, reading-related literature, and challenge or extension exercises. Using cloze procedures, working puzzles, and labeling diagrams are examples of the activities used. The lessons are not presented sequentially. No lesson is dependent on any that precede it.

Each lesson has 11 words. We encourage you to add words or to have students add words which are frequently missed in their own spelling. The additional words for the class could include spelling demons or content words related to the topic in the lesson.

USE

The lessons and activities are designed for independent use by learners as large groups, small groups, or individuals. An introduction of the words is recommended, with dialogue to ensure comprehension of the word meanings.

1. <u>Give</u> a pre-test using the suggested assessment tool found on page 97.
2. <u>Identify</u> a lesson with content relevant to other curriculum currently being studied. Duplicate the three-page lesson for the learners.
3. <u>Develop</u> a plan for implementation. A sample plan includes a pre-test and distribution of page 1 of the lesson on Monday, completion of activities on page 1 on Tuesday, completion of activities on pages 2 and 3 on Wednesday and Thursday, and a post-test on Friday.
4. <u>Determine</u> additional words. Spelling demons are listed on page 97. Give the words orally as a pre-test.
5. <u>Introduce</u> the words to the learners. Clarify directions to activities.

ADDITIONAL NOTES

1. <u>Student Paper</u>. Students use their own paper to alphabetize the words in each lesson.
2. <u>Parent Communication</u>. Send the Letter to Parents home with the students. This letter offers suggestions for parental involvement to increase learner success.
3. <u>Small Groups</u>. Small group activities are included in many lessons. Identify the procedures for formation of the groups.
4. <u>Misspelled Words - Class Record</u>. A record of the frequently misspelled words by the class can be maintained on page 3. The page could be duplicated for students to keep individual records. These words can be added to other word lists to ensure mastery.
5. <u>Have fun</u>. The activities are cross-curricular and use a variety of strategies to maintain student interest. Watch your students' spelling improve as words are applied in structured, relevant practice!

© Steck-Vaughn Company

Spelling 6, SV 6747-6

MISSPELLED WORDS
Class Record Sheet

Unit I. Social Studies	
Industrial Revolution	
Geography	
Election/Government	
Ancient Times	
Coming to America	
Mexico	
Unit II. Art	
Impressionism	
Architecture	
Unit III. P.E.	
Health	
Sports	
Unit IV. Music	
Music & Dance of Mexico	
Terms	
Unit V. Science	
Laboratory Equipment	
Human Body	
Technology	
Chemistry	
Heredity	
Astronomy	
Unit VI. Language Arts	
Gary Paulsen/*Hatchet*	
Paragraphs	
Kinds of Literature	
Research Paper	
Journal Writing	
Media	
Unit VII. Math	
Probability/Statistics	
Graphs	
Pre-Algebra	
Geometry	
Money	
Tools/Terms	

Dear Parent,

During this school year, our class will be working with a spelling program that uses a thematic approach to word study skills. To increase your child's spelling skills, we will be completing activity sheets that provide practice to ensure mastery of these important skills.

From time to time, I may send home activity sheets. To best help your child, please consider the following suggestions:

- Provide a quiet place to work.
- Go over the directions and the words together.
- Review the words frequently for both spelling and meaning.
- Help your child find the words in the context by using newspapers or other reading material.
- Make up word games.
- Encourage your child to do his or her best.
- Check the lesson when it is complete.
- Go over your child's work and note improvements as well as concerns.

Help your child maintain a positive attitude about spelling skills. Let your child know that each lesson provides an opportunity to have fun and to learn. If your child expresses anxiety about these skills, help him or her understand what causes the stress. Then talk about ways to deal with spelling anxiety.

Above all, enjoy this time you spend with your child. He or she will feel your support, and skills will improve with each activity completed.

Thank you for your help!

Cordially,

Name_____ Date_____

Social Studies
Industrial Revolution p. 1

WORD LIST
- textiles
- factories
- labor
- revolution
- products
- industry
- machines
- transportation
- wages
- efficient
- inventions

Write these words in alphabetical order on a separate sheet of paper. Remember, if more than one word begins with the same letter, look at the second, third, or maybe fourth letter in each word.

1. Write the words that begin with vowels.

   _____ _____
   _____

2. Write the words in the correct columns.

   2-syllable words **3-syllable words** **4-syllable words**

3. Write the word that formed the plural by changing **y** to **i** and adding **es**.

   _____

Try This Many things that we take for granted are the inventions of people who wanted to make life a little easier. For example, consider how the invention of the sewing machine was a great help to the clothing industry. Look around your house. Did people always have a toaster to make toast? Brainstorm and make a list of inventions that have made easier the way things are done. Try to list the date of each invention.

Extension The Industrial Revolution began in England around 1750. Through research, create a pictorial time line showing important inventions up through the 1900s. Choose the invention that you think made the most impact on the world and write why. Share and discuss papers with your classmates.

Name _____ Date _____

Social Studies
Industrial Revolution p. 2

WORD LIST
- textiles
- factories
- labor
- revolution
- products
- industry
- machines
- transportation
- wages
- efficient
- inventions

Find the word in the Word List that best fits each clue. Then use the numbered letters to find the name of an important invention made during the Industrial Revolution.

1. Pay for work done __ __₈ __ __ __ __
2. Work __₁₁ __ __ __ __
3. Capable, practical __ __ __ __₁₄ __ __ __ __ __
4. Way of getting from one place to another __ __ __ __ __ __₆ __ __ __ __ __ __ __ __
5. Places where things are made __ __₄ __₁₂ __ __ __ __ __ __
6. Cloth, material __ __ __₃ __ __ __ __ __
7. Things made __ __ __ __₁₀ __ __ __ __
8. Business __ __ __ __ __ __₉ __ __
9. Framework used for making things __ __₅ __ __ __ __ __ __
10. A great change __ __ __ __ __ __₇ __ __ __₂ __
11. New methods or devices __ __ __ __ __ __ __ __ __₁₃ __ __ __ __₁ __

Secret words __₁ __₂ __₃ __₄ __₅ __₆ __₇ __₈ __₃ __₉ __₃ __₁₀

__₁₁ __₇ __₁₂ __₇ __₅ __₇ __₂ __₁₄ __₁₃ __₃

LET'S WRITE Think about what changes came about because of the invention you decoded above. Write a paragraph describing the changes that took place. Use at least 5 words from the Word List. Then, write another paragraph explaining what effect that invention had on other inventions.

Name_____ Date _____

Social Studies
Industrial Revolution p. 3

Word List
- textiles
- factories
- labor
- revolution
- products
- industry
- machines
- transportation
- wages
- efficient
- inventions

Label the pictures with words from the Word List.

_____

_____

Complete the passage with words from the Word List.

Benjamin Franklin, besides being a writer and a historian, was also responsible for many ❶_____, such as bifocals, the lightning rod, and what is known as the Franklin stove. Although these inventions may not seem as monumental as the steam engine, they did help people by making things better. Some inventions, like the steam engine, brought about big changes. Owners of ❷_____ where people worked now had powerful new ❸_____ that helped them turn out their ❹_____, or wares quickly. In many cases the machines were more ❺_____ and would make fewer mistakes than people. These machines could do the work of many people. The invention and inclusion of machines brought about a ❻_____, a great change, in the way an ❼_____, or business, did things. Because of machines, much of the ❽_____ was now done mechanically. Some people lost their jobs, and as a result, they lost ❾_____, which were used to pay for other things.

What do you think would have happened if there had been no such thing as the Industrial Revolution?

....

Let's read these "inventive" books.
Ranch Dressing: The Story of Western Wear by M. Jean Greenlaw
The Smithsonian Visual Timeline of Inventions by Richard Platt

Name_____ Date _____

Social Studies
Geography p. 1

WORD LIST
- deserts
- arctic
- antarctic
- temperatures
- harsh
- equator
- evaporate
- adapt
- precipitation
- dunes
- formation

Write these words in alphabetical order on a separate sheet of paper. Remember, if more than one word begins with the same letter, look at the second, third, or maybe fourth letter in each word.

1. Write the words that are plural.
   _____ _____ _____

2. Write the words that end with the suffix **-tion**.
   _____ _____

3. Write the words that have the **ar** sound.
   _____ _____ _____

4. Write the words that begin with **ē** sound.
   _____ _____

5. Write the words with 2 syllables.
   _____ _____ _____

Try This

Did you know that there are both hot and cold deserts? Scientists define deserts as areas of land where less than ten inches of rain falls in a year and few plants can grow. There are cold areas where this is the case. Find the names of 5 hot deserts and identify their locations. See if you can find out where the cold deserts are located.

Name_____ Date _____

Social Studies
Geography p. 2

Complete the puzzle with words from the Word List.

WORD LIST
- deserts
- arctic
- antarctic
- temperatures
- harsh
- equator
- evaporate
- adapt
- precipitation
- dunes
- formation

Across:
1. Near the South Pole
2. Rain or snow
6. Sand hills
8. Vaporize
9. Regions where little rain falls
10. Way something is shaped

Down:
1. Adjust
3. Imaginary circle around earth
4. Degrees of hotness or coldness
5. Extremely cold
7. Ruthless or unkind

 Write the beginning of a science fiction story in which the only places left to live are the cold and/or hot deserts. Survivors now have to start a new life in these areas. Use at least 5 words from the Word List. Remember, this is just a beginning. Define your setting and your characters.

 Let's Read these "chilling" books.
Troubling a Star by Madeleine L'Engle
Frozen Land by Jan Reynolds

Name_____ Date_____

Social Studies
Geography p. 3

WORD LIST
- deserts
- arctic
- antarctic
- temperatures
- harsh
- equator
- evaporate
- adapt
- precipitation
- dunes
- formation

Label the picture with words from the Word List.

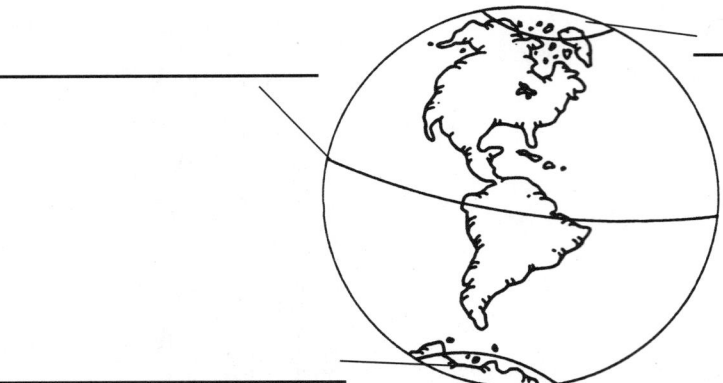

Complete the passage with words from the Word List.

The ❶_____ are large and barren places

Where ❷_____, like rain, leaves merely traces.

And even when the rain falls fast,

It will ❸_____, or dry up. It doesn't last!

The ❹_____ are extremely hot or cold.

Conditions are ❺_____ and cruel, I'm told.

The plants and animals ❻_____ to these extremes.

They find amazing ways to survive, it seems.

There are ❼_____, or hills of sand

That make an interesting ❽_____ on the land.

If traveling through a sand desert for fun.

Beware and be careful of the very hot sun!

....

Extension Research hot and cold deserts. Take notes on what you read. Using your notes, finish the science fiction story that you started under Let's Write. Remember what you have read about animals adapting to their environment. In your story, human survivors have to adapt to living in extreme hot or cold conditions. Share your story with the class. Don't forget to develop the plot.

Name_____ Date _____

Social Studies
Election/Government p. 1

WORD LIST
- campaign
- politics
- candidate
- party
- issues
- election
- speech
- support
- vote
- leaders
- integrity

Write these words in alphabetical order on a separate sheet of paper. Remember, if more than one word begins with the same letter, look at the second, third, or maybe fourth letter in each word.

1. Write the words that contain a double consonant or double vowel.

   _____ _____

   _____

2. Write the words that end with the ē sound for the letter **y**.

   _____ _____

3. Write the words with 3 syllables.

   _____ _____

   _____

4. Write the words with 1 syllable.

   _____ _____

5. Write the word that contains a silent **g**.

   _____

6. Write the words that mean more than one.

   _____ _____

 Integrity is one quality of a good leader. List at least 5 other qualities that you would like a leader to possess. Next to each quality, write the name of a leader you think possesses that quality. Use a different name for each quality and explain why you think this person exemplifies the trait. Share your list and names with the class.

Social Studies
Election/Government p. 2

Complete the puzzle with words from the Word List.

WORD LIST
- campaign
- politics
- candidate
- party
- issues
- election
- speech
- support
- vote
- leaders
- integrity

Across:
2. A choice by vote
3. Person running for office
5. Talk given to an audience
6. Group of people promoting a cause
7. Points being discussed
9. The science of government
10. Honesty

Down:
1. Cast a ballot
3. Plans for electing a candidate
4. Persons who lead
8. To stand behind

 You are running for "Class President." Write a speech explaining why you are the best person for the job. Use at least 5 words from the Word List. Have a mock election day when you all share your speeches and have the class vote for a "Class President."

 Let's Read these books about leaders.
Presidents of a Growing Country edited by Carter Smith
Presidents Almanac by Kessler & Segal

Name_____   Date_____

Social Studies
Election/Government p. 3

WORD LIST
- campaign
- politics
- candidate
- party
- issues
- election
- speech
- support
- vote
- leaders
- integrity

Complete the passage with words from the Word List.

The science of government, or ❶_____, can be very interesting. Every four years the United States holds an ❷_____ for President of the United States. Everyone is encouraged to ❸_____, or cast a ballot, for the ❹_____ he or she thinks will make the best president. During a candidate's ❺_____, people are able to hear the ❻_____, or concerns, discussed and sometimes debated. The ❼_____ of a political ❽_____ will go out and try to get people to ❾_____, or stand behind, their chosen candidate. Many times, a party leader will give a ❿_____ telling listeners why they should vote for a person. Before voting for a candidate, a person should make sure that the candidate has a great deal of ⓫_____, or honesty.

Extension   Choose a past president who interests you. Research that person's climb to the presidency. Create a historical time line using pictures and facts to show the accomplishments of this person during his lifetime. Display and share your time line with the class.

Name_____ Date_____

Social Studies
Ancient Times p. 1

Write these words in alphabetical order on a separate sheet of paper. Remember, if more than one word begins with the same letter, look at the second, third, or maybe fourth letter in each word.

WORD LIST
- civilization
- flourish
- society
- ancient
- artifacts
- explore
- archaeology
- ruins
- vanished
- temples
- monuments

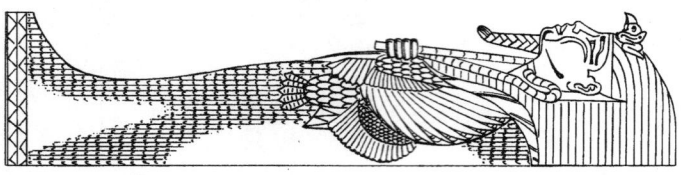

1. Write the words that are plural.

   _____ _____
   _____ _____

2. Write the words that end with the ē sound for the letter **y**.

   _____ _____

3. Write the words that contain the **sh** sound.

   _____ _____ _____

4. Write the words with 2 syllables.

   _____ _____ _____
   _____ _____ _____

Write the heading *Ancient Times* on a sheet of paper. Then list as many things as you can that you believe reflect ancient times. Write for about 5 minutes. Get together as a class and make a master list. Once the list is made, try to find out which ancient civilization may have been the first to make or do each item on your list. Locate on a globe where these people once lived.

Design and write a full-page Help Wanted ad for someone to join you on an archaeological dig. In the ad tell where you will be going, what you will be looking for, and why you think this would be an interesting job. Use at least 6 words from the Word List in your ad. Display the ads around the classroom.

Name_____ Date_____

Social Studies
Ancient Times p. 2

Word List
- civilization
- flourish
- society
- ancient
- artifacts
- explore
- archaeology
- ruins
- vanished
- temples
- monuments

Complete the analogies with words from the Word List.

1. New is to modern as old is to _____.
2. Stars are to astronomy as _____ are to _____.
3. Righted is to corrected as disappeared is to _____.
4. Extinct is to bygone as _____ is to thrive.
5. Find is to discover as search is to _____.
6. Primitive is to undeveloped as _____ is to developed.

Complete the puzzle with words from the Word List.

Across:
1. Objects made by humans
3. Structures set up in memory of people

Down:
2. Places of worship
4. Group of people

Let's Read these "ancient" books.
Ancient Egypt (Journey Into Civilization) by Nicholson & Watts
Ancient Egyptians: Life in the Nile Valley by Viviane Koenig

Extension   Research and create a pictorial time line showing important events from 300 to 1500 B.C. Use books and materials found on the computer to help create your time line. If possible, work with a partner. Display your time line.

Name_____ Date _____

Social Studies
Ancient Times p. 3

WORD LIST
- civilization
- flourish
- society
- ancient
- artifacts
- explore
- archaeology
- ruins
- vanished
- temples
- monuments

Complete the passage with words from the Word List.

The beginning of ❶_____ is said to have been around 5000 BC. It was at this time that people began to live together. In other words, a group of people formed a ❷_____. In the science of ❸_____, people dig up ❹_____ from old, or ❺_____, civilizations and study them. By studying these artifacts, scientists can tell what kinds of tools, food, and homes these ancient people might have had. Sometimes ❻_____ of entire cities that had once ❼_____, or disappeared, are uncovered. Archaeologists can study what helped the people ❽_____, or thrive. Ruins of ❾_____, or places of worship, have been uncovered. Sometimes these ruins can tell what the people worshiped. Tablets, statues, and other ❿_____ have also been uncovered. These artifacts can tell much about a people. Monuments like the pyramids were build as tombs for the kings. Imagine what it would be like to ⓫_____ one of the ancient pyramids.

What do you think you would find in one of the ancient pyramids? Write a short story about the discovery and exploration of a lost pyramid. You can make your story a mystery.

Name_____ Date _____

Social Studies
Coming to America p. 1

WORD LIST
- establish
- toils
- opportunity
- dangers
- comfort
- risking
- voyage
- immigrants
- embark
- depart
- potential

Write these words in alphabetical order on a separate sheet of paper. Remember, if more than one word begins with the same letter, look at the second, third, or maybe fourth letter in each word.

1. Write the words that are plural.

   _____   _____

   _____

2. Write the words that contain 3 syllables.

   _____   _____

3. Write the words that contain 2 syllables.

   _____   _____

   _____   _____

   _____

4. Write the word that ends with the **ē** sound for the letter **y**. _____

 Make a flag that represents the country or countries from which your family members originally came. Find out at least 5 facts about the country or countries to share with the class. For example, if your grandparents originally came from Ireland and Italy, you would make the flags for these countries and list 5 facts about each country.

 Write a story about your ancestors' immigration. Interview your parents and other family members to learn about the country or countries from which they originally came. Find out what toils or dangers they might have encountered on their trip. If you can't gather this information from family members, write how you think your family traveled here, and what toils and dangers were met. If your ancestors are Native Americans, write about what this country was like and how the arrival of the immigrants may have affected their lives. Share your research and report with the class. Use at least 6 words from the Word List.

© Steck-Vaughn Company   Spelling 6 SV 6747-6

Name_____ Date _____

Social Studies
Coming to America p. 2

WORD LIST
- establish
- toils
- opportunity
- dangers
- comfort
- risking
- voyage
- immigrants
- embark
- depart
- potential

Read each clue. Write the word from the Word List that best fits each clue.

1. Struggles, work _____
2. Leave, exit _____
3. Trip by sea _____
4. Break, chance _____
5. Possibility, ability _____
6. Begin, start to go _____
7. Perils, hazards _____
8. Foreigners, aliens _____
9. Peace, contentment _____
10. Found, initiate _____
11. Taking chances _____

 Let's Read these books about immigrants.
One-Way to Ansonia by Judie Angell
Hector Lives in the United States Now by Joan Hewett

Extension   Help plan a multi-cultural day for your class. Share your stories with the class. Display the flags that you made in the *Try This* activity. You might want to make a multi-cultural cookbook. Bring in one or two recipes that are "old family recipes." For each recipe, write the story of how it came to be a part of your family. Publish the cookbook and make a copy for everyone in the class.

Name_____ Date _____

Social Studies
Coming to America p. 3

WORD LIST
- establish
- toils
- opportunity
- dangers
- comfort
- risking
- voyage
- immigrants
- embark
- depart
- potential

Complete the passage with words from the Word List.

People who come from other countries to live in America are known as ❶_____. In the 1840s there were many Irish and German immigrants who came to America to ❷_____, or create, new lives for themselves. These people left the ❸_____ of their homes and families to ❹_____, or begin, their journey to America. They had much to do even before they could ❺_____, or leave. They had to plan and pack for the long ❻_____ across the sea. These people may not have known they were ❼_____ their very lives pursuing what they felt was a great ❽_____, or chance, to start a new life. While on the voyage, these people encountered many ❾_____ such as storms and rough seas. Once these people reached the shores of America, they encountered other struggles, or ❿_____, which made their lives very difficult. The ⓫_____, or ability to achieve, the peace and comfort they longed for seemed to be out of their reach. But they survived their struggles. They helped make America become known as a "melting pot" of people, and they helped it become the country it is today.

What do you think it was like to travel across the sea from Europe to America in the 1700s and 1800s? Imagine that you are on such a voyage. Write a journal entry describing 1 day.

Name_____ Date_____

Social Studies
Mexico p. 1

WORD LIST
- neighbor
- lariat
- border
- exports
- sombrero
- poncho
- cocoa
- fiesta
- adobe
- piñata
- maize

Write these words in alphabetical order on a separate sheet of paper. Remember, if more than one word begins with the same letter, look at the second, third, or maybe fourth letter in each word.

1. Write the words that end with a vowel sound.

   _____ _____
   _____ _____
   _____

2. Write the words with the **or** sound.

   _____ _____
   _____

3. Write the words with **ā** sound.

   _____ _____

4. Write the words in which the letter **i** has the **ē** sound.

   _____ _____

Several of the words in the Word List are words you would hear if you visited Mexico. There are other words that we hear and/or use that come from our neighbor to the south of the United States. Brainstorm and make a list of those words. Think of foods we eat, clothing we wear, and expressions that we might use, such as *adios*, which means "good-bye." Try to list at least 10 words. Then, as a class, combine all the lists to see how many different words you have discovered. Keep the list displayed in the room.

Let's Read these books about our neighbors.
Mexico, Giant of the South by Eileen Larell Smith
Beyond the Ancient Cities by Jose Maria Merino

© Steck-Vaughn Company   20   Spelling 6, SV 6747-6

Name_____ Date _____

Social Studies
Mexico p. 2

Complete the puzzle with words from the Word List.

WORD LIST
- neighbor
- lariat
- border
- exports
- sombrero
- poncho
- cocoa
- fiesta
- adobe
- piñata
- maize

Across:
1. Hot chocolate
6. Wide-brimmed hat
7. Boundary
8. Goods shipped out
10. Person next door
11. Corn

Down:
2. Red clay brick
3. Worn to keep warm or dry
4. Rope
5. Party or celebration
9. Decorated container filled with surprises

LET'S WRITE You have just been on vacation to Mexico. Write a letter to a friend describing what you did and what you saw. Use at least 5 words from the Word List. You might also want to design a post card using one of more of the items listed in the Word List. Share your letter and post card with the class.

Extension Research ancient Mexico. Find out about the Mayan and Aztec empires. Find out about their rich art and architecture. Use books and pictures to find their influences. Write a report to share with the class.

Social Studies
Mexico p. 3

WORD LIST
- neighbor
- lariat
- border
- exports
- sombrero
- poncho
- cocoa
- fiesta
- adobe
- piñata
- maize

Label the pictures with words from the Word List.

Complete the passage with words from the Word List.

Our ❶_____ to the south of the United States and just across the ❷_____ is Mexico. Mexico has had many influences here in the United States. In the southwestern states, you can see homes that are built with ❸_____, or red baked clay bricks. In many states, Mexican influences can be seen, heard, and felt during special times when people are celebrating their Mexican heritage. A festival or celebration is called a ❹_____.

Oil is one of Mexico's largest ❺_____, or goods shipped out. Mexico is one of the largest oil exporters. Only about 15% of the land is suitable for farming. In a country that is 761,600 square miles, that is not a lot of land.

Why is only 15% of the land suitable for farming? Research to find out the answer.

Name_____ Date _____

Art
impressionism (Monet & Van Gogh) p. 1

WORD LIST
- distinctive
- style
- vivid
- texture
- marvels
- influence
- critics
- image
- vibrant
- tragic
- depressed

Write these words in alphabetical order on a separate sheet of paper. Remember, if more than one word begins with the same letter, look at the second, third, or maybe fourth letter in each word.

....

1. Write the words in the correct columns.

   2-syllable words   **3-syllable words**

   _____   _____
   _____   _____
   _____
   _____
   _____
   _____
   _____

2. Write the words in which the letter **g** has the **j** sound.

   _____   _____

3. Write the word in which the letter **y** has the **ī** sound.

   _____

....

Find out about Monet, Van Gogh, and impressionism. As you read about these artists and their style of art, list at least 6 other words that tell about the artists' lives, their art, and the period of impressionism.

Choose a painting by either Monet or Van Gogh. Study the painting. Write a review of the painting using at least 5 words from the Word List. To get an idea of how to write an art review, check your Sunday newspaper in the arts section for examples. Share a picture of the painting and your review with the class.

Name_____ Date _____

Art
impressionism (Monet & Van Gogh) p. 2

WORD LIST
- distinctive
- style
- vivid
- texture
- marvels
- influence
- critics
- image
- vibrant
- tragic
- depressed

Complete the analogies with words from the Word List.

1. <u>Dark</u> is to <u>dull</u> as <u>bright</u> is to _____,

   or _____ .

2. <u>Common</u> is to <u>ordinary</u> as <u>special</u> is to

   _____ .

3. <u>Happy</u> is to <u>carefree</u> as <u>sad</u> is to

   _____ , or _____ .

4. <u>Aroma</u> is to <u>smell</u> as _____ is to <u>feel</u>.

Use the words from the Word List to complete the puzzle.

Across:
1. Power to sway
3. Spectacles, wonders

Down:
1. Likeness
2. Judges
4. Technique

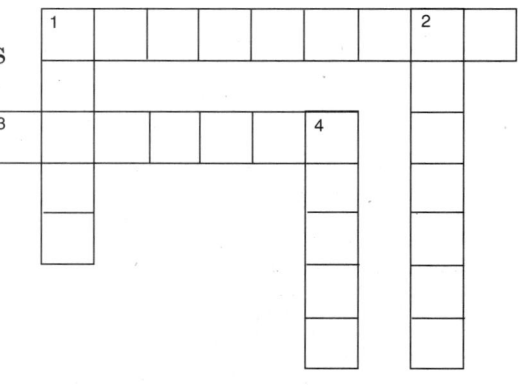

 Let's Read these colorful books.
Painting: A Young Artist's Guide by Annie Harris and Elizabeth Waters
A Brush with Magic by William Brooke

Extension   Choose 2 other artists of the impressionistic period to research. Gather notes about their lives and their individual painting styles. Write a comparison of these 2 artists. Tell how they are alike and how they are different. If possible, find a copy or a picture of a painting by each of them. Share your report with the class.

Art
impressionism (Monet & Van Gogh) p. 3

WORD LIST
- distinctive
- style
- vivid
- texture
- marvels
- influence
- critics
- image
- vibrant
- tragic
- depressed

Complete the passage with words from the Word List.

The artists Monet and Van Gogh were both considered impressionists. Each of them, however, had a ❶_____, or special, ❷_____, or technique. Monet wanted to show the ❸_____, or wonders, of the real world. He painted wonderful gardens. He dabbed the paint on the canvas. When you stand close to a painting by Monet, the ❹_____, or likeness, might seem blurred. You must stand back to see the image clearly. Impressionism did ❺_____, or sway, Van Gogh in his early stages of painting. However, Van Gogh later used ❻_____ and ❼_____ colors in his paintings. In his painting, *The Starry Night*, he uses brilliant purples, blues, and yellows. In Van Gogh's paintings, you can see and feel the ❽_____ of the paint. He used ridges of thick paint to make some lines stand out more.

Both artists became ❾_____, or melancholy, over the comments expressed by ❿_____. Both were unable to sell their paintings, and as a result, both went without food and gathered large debts. Van Gogh could not cope with these setbacks. In a ⓫_____ turn, he took his own life. Today, both his paintings and those of Monet are displayed in museums and sell for millions of dollars each!

Name_____ Date _____

Art
Architecture (Frank Lloyd Wright) p. 1

WORD LIST
- modern
- designed
- materials
- complemented
- landscape
- inspired
- natural
- spacious
- harmonized
- architect
- traditions

Write these words in alphabetical order on a separate sheet of paper. Remember, if more than one word begins with the same letter, look at the second, third, or maybe fourth letter in each word.

1. Write the words that form the past tense using **-ed**.

   _____   _____

   _____   _____

2. Write the plural words.

   _____   _____

3. Write the word that ends with the letter **s**, but is not plural.

   _____

4. Write the words that contain the **er** sound.

   _____   _____

5. Write the words that have a silent letter.

   _____   _____

   _____

6. Write the 2-syllable word that has both the **ă** and **ā** sound.

   _____

Brainstorm and list the skills that an architect needs to possess. Explain why each of the skills is necessary and how it helps an architect. Then explain what might happen if we did not have architects.

After looking at pictures of Frank Lloyd Wright homes, write a real estate ad for a house designed by this architect. Use at least 5 words from the Word List. To get a feel for real estate ads, look in the real estate section of a newspaper.

Name_____ Date_____

Art
Architecture (Frank Lloyd Wright) p. 2

WORD LIST
- modern
- designed
- materials
- complemented
- landscape
- inspired
- natural
- spacious
- harmonized
- architect
- traditions

Complete the analogies with words from the Word List.

1. <u>Story</u> is to <u>author</u> as <u>building</u> is to _____.

2. <u>Small</u> is to <u>confined</u> as <u>vast</u> is to _____.

3. <u>Old</u> is to <u>outdated</u> as <u>new</u> is to _____.

4. <u>Artificial</u> is to <u>manmade</u> as <u>real</u> is to _____.

5. <u>Tired</u> is to <u>repetitive</u> as <u>fresh</u> is to _____.

Use the words from the Word List to complete the puzzle.

Across:
2. Completed or perfected
4. Natural scenery
6. Pleasing effect

Down:
1. Formed a plan
3. Tools and supplies
5. Certain ways of doing things

Let's Read these well-designed books.
Frank Lloyd Wright by Yona Zeldis McDonough
A Short Walk Around the Pyramids and through the World of Art by Philip M. Isaacson

Extension Frank Lloyd Wright was a man "ahead of his time." Think about what this means. Find at least 3 examples of others who could be considered "ahead of their time." Share your findings with the class.

Art
Architecture (Frank Lloyd Wright) p. 3

WORD LIST
- modern
- designed
- materials
- complemented
- landscape
- inspired
- natural
- spacious
- harmonized
- architect
- traditions

Complete the passage with words from the Word List.

Frank Lloyd Wright was an ❶_____ and an artist. He ❷_____ and created a series of houses called "prairie homes." The design of these homes was ❸_____ by his love of nature. He made sure the homes ❹_____, or perfected, the ❺_____ surroundings in which the houses were to be built. The homes were built so they would not disturb the ❻_____, or surrounding scenery. He used ❼_____ that emphasized his love of nature. He used wood for floors and ceilings and made sure there were plenty of windows to give even small rooms a ❽_____ look.

Another house designed and built by this architect is called "Falling Water." The house was built almost 60 years ago and is considered to be very ❾_____, even for its time. With this house, Wright ❿_____, or brought together, nature and manmade materials so that it all looks natural. There are architects today who still try to follow the ⓫_____, or ways, of Frank Lloyd Wright. His houses are truly "art forms" to be seen and admired.

P.E.
Health p. 1

WORD LIST
- disease
- infectious
- epidemic
- viral
- contagious
- bacterial
- transmitted
- antibiotics
- injection
- prescription
- vaccine

Write these words in alphabetical order on a separate sheet of paper. Remember, if more than one word begins with the same letter, look at the second, third, or maybe fourth letter in each word.

1. Write the words in the correct columns.

   2-syllable words   **3-syllable words**

   _____   _____
   _____   _____
   _____   _____
                                 _____
   4-syllable words   _____

   _____   **5-syllable word**
   _____   _____

2. Write the words that contain a double consonant.

   _____   _____

3. Write the words that end with the suffix **-tion**.

   _____   _____

4. Write the words that end with the suffix **-ious**.

   _____   _____

TRY THIS

Brainstorm and make a list of at least 5 common infectious diseases, such as the common cold. Next to each disease identify whether it is a virus or a bacteria and how the disease is transmitted. For example, the common cold is a virus and it is transmitted through contact with an infected person. Find out the best care or

Name _____ Date _____

P.E.
Health p. 2

WORD LIST
- disease
- infectious
- epidemic
- viral
- contagious
- bacterial
- transmitted
- antibiotics
- injection
- prescription
- vaccine

Write the word from the Word List that best fits each clue.

1. Caused by a virus _____
2. Illness _____
3. Passed on _____
4. Caused by a bacteria _____
5. Easily transmitted _____
6. Illness spreading rapidly _____
7. Written direction for a medicine _____
8. Medicine given by needle _____
9. Spread by contact _____
10. Substances used to destroy bacteria _____
11. Substance used to produce immunity _____

LET'S WRITE You have just made a medical breakthrough. You have found a cure for a disease. Write an article for a medical journal (in your own words) telling about your discovery. Remember to answer the questions who, what, why, how, where, and when. Use at least 5 words from the Word List.

 Let's Read these books.
My Brother Has AIDS by Deborah Davis
The Legacy: Making Wishes Come True by Lurlene McDaniel

Extension Research to find out more about the field of medicine and who some of the people were who made us more aware of diseases. For example, find out who discovered the vaccine against polio and when the vaccine became available. Find out how the vaccine helped to control this deadly disease. Make a medicine time line showing important discoveries.

P.E.
Health p. 3

WORD LIST
- disease
- infectious
- epidemic
- viral
- contagious
- bacterial
- transmitted
- antibiotics
- injection
- prescription
- vaccine

Complete the passage with words from the Word List.

Microscopic organisms that enter the body can cause what we know as an ❶_____ ❷_____. This means that the illness can be passed on, or ❸_____, through contact. These infectious diseases are called communicable, or ❹_____, diseases. When a contagious disease spreads rapidly and infects many people, it is know as an ❺_____. One terrifying epidemic was The Black Death epidemic of the 1300s. This disease killed more than 60 million people.

Diseases or illnesses that are caused by bacteria, such as Lyme disease or whooping cough, are known as ❻_____ diseases. Bacterial diseases can be treated with ❼_____, such as penicillin. These drugs slow the growth of bacteria and kill them without killing the body's cells. You can only get these drugs with a ❽_____ from your doctor. Antibiotics can be given by ❾_____ in the doctor's office or in pill form. Antibiotics are not helpful in treating ❿_____ infections. These infections are caused by viruses. To strengthen the body's immunity against certain viruses, such as measles or chicken pox, doctors have developed what is known as a ⓫_____. This medicine is given orally or through an injection. Check with your parents to see what vaccinations you have had.

Name_____ Date _____

P.E.
Sports p. 1

WORD LIST
- racquet
- tennis
- opponent
- server
- boundaries
- singles
- doubles
- deuce
- court
- points
- match

Write these words in alphabetical order on a separate sheet of paper. Remember, if more than one word begins with the same letter, look at the second, third, or maybe fourth letter in each word.

1. Write the words that are plural.

   _____ _____
   _____ _____

2. Write the words that contain a double consonant.

   _____ _____

3. Write the words with the **ă** sound.

   _____ _____

4. Write the one-syllable words.

   _____ _____
   _____ _____

5. Write the word that has the **er** sound in both syllables.

   _____

 Brainstorm and list other words you associate with the sport of tennis. Once you have the list, write how you think tennis is played. Do this without looking up the sport in any reference materials. Share your instructions for playing the game. Then check reference materials for how the game is really played. Compare your instructions with the actual instructions.

 Have you ever watched a tennis game being played? Have you ever watched fans watching the game of tennis being played? Think about these ideas. Jot down what comes to mind. Take your notes and write a poem using at least 5 words from the Word List.

P.E.
Sports p. 2

WORD LIST
- racquet
- tennis
- opponent
- server
- boundaries
- singles
- doubles
- deuce
- court
- points
- match

Complete the puzzle with words from the Word List.

Across:
3. Borders
6. Ones
8. One who serves
9. Playing field for tennis
11. 1 game of tennis

Down:
1. Twos
2. Game played with racquet and ball
4. Tool used to hit ball in tennis
5. Scores
7. Tie score
10. Player on opposite side

Let's Read these "sporty" books.
Wimbledon by Nancy Gilbert
Soccer Circus: Featuring Hobie Hanson by Jamie Gilson

Extension What do you think it takes to be really good or even great at a sport? Write a recipe for how to be a champion. For example, how much stamina does it take? How much dedication? How much practice? How much strength? Think of all the qualities that go into making a champion. Share your recipe for being a champion with the class.

P.E.
Sports p. 3

WORD LIST
- racquet
- tennis
- opponent
- server
- boundaries
- singles
- doubles
- deuce
- court
- points
- match

Label the picture with words from the Word List.

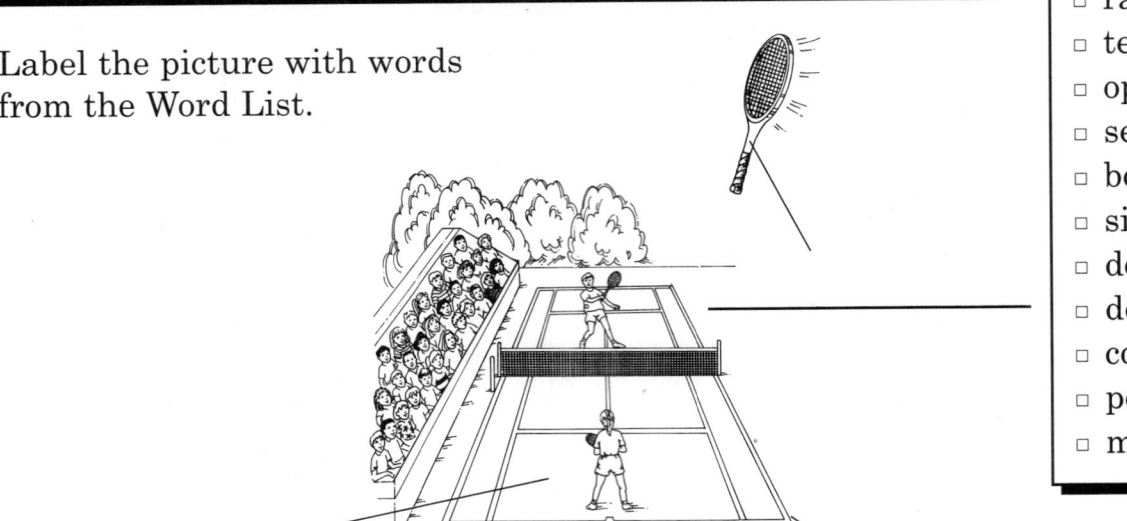

Complete the passage with words from the Word List.

The game played by hitting a ball over the net with a racquet is called ❶_____ . Tennis is an all-season game because it can be played both indoors and outdoors. Games played between two people are called ❷_____ . Games played between four people, with two people on each team, are called ❸_____. The game played is called a ❹_____ . Why? It may be because the players are matched up. The player who begins the play by hitting the ball is the ❺_____. The server hits the ball to the player on the other side of the net. This player is called the ❻_____. A player can earn ❼_____ by making the other player miss the ball. When the score is tied, it is called ❽_____ . Four points wins the game. Whoever wins six games first wins the set. A match consists of the best of three sets for women, and the best of five sets for men. Find the names of four tennis players who have been Wimbledon Champions.

Name_____ Date_____

Music
Music & Dance of Mexico p. 1

WORD LIST
- mariachi
- strolling
- ranchero
- accordion
- emotion
- folk
- costumes
- blending
- cultures
- horns
- guitarists

Write these words in alphabetical order on a separate sheet of paper. Remember, if more than one word begins with the same letter, look at the second, third, or maybe fourth letter in each word.

1. Write the words that are plural.

   _____ _____

   _____ _____

2. Write the words that have the suffix **-ing**.

   _____ _____

3. Write the words that begin with a vowel.

   _____

   _____

4. Write the words that end with a vowel.

   _____ _____

5. Write the words without double consonants that have a silent letter.

   _____

TRY THIS — Find and list the names of at least 5 different folk dances and the countries from which they originate. For example, the *jarabe tapatito*, or the Mexican hat dance, is a lively dance that is performed in villages as well as the Palace of Fine Arts in Mexico City. List at least 3 facts about each dance. This can include when it is danced, what costumes are worn, and what meaning the dance might have. Share your findings with the class. If you find a recording of the music, bring it to class to share.

LET'S WRITE — Ranchero music is sung by ranch hands in Mexico. How does this music compare with any music in the United States? What music might ranch hands in the United States sing? Write a brief explanation of how ranchero music might be a blending of cultures. Use at least 5 words from the Word List. You might want to look up music of Mexico to find out more about it.

Name_____ Date _____

Music
Music & Dance of Mexico p. 2

WORD LIST
- mariachi
- strolling
- ranchero
- accordion
- emotion
- folk
- costumes
- blending
- cultures
- horns
- guitarists

Complete the puzzle with words from the Word List.

Across:
3. Colorful clothes
5. Group of strolling musicians
9. Spanish for *ranch*
10. Skills, arts, etc. of a people
11. People who play the guitar

Down:
1. Musical instrument
2. Feeling
4. Slowly walking
6. Trumpets
7. Mixing together
8. Common to the people

 Let's Read these books.
Mexican Ghost Tales of the Southwest by Alfred Avila
The Hummingbirds' Gift by Stefan Czernecki

Extension Choose a style of music that you like. It could be rock and roll, country, classical, or any other style. Research the music and find out where it got its beginnings. You will be surprised how far back some of the music roots go. Bring in a favorite piece. Be ready to explain why you like the music style in general and why the particular piece is a favorite of yours. You can have your own music awards show.

Name_____ Date_____

Music
Music & Dance of Mexico p. 3

WORD LIST
- mariachi
- strolling
- ranchero
- accordion
- emotion
- folk
- costumes
- blending
- cultures
- horns
- guitarists

Label the pictures with words from the Word List.

Complete the passage with words from the Word List.

Music can get my feet to tapping,

Whether its ❶_____ or country or even rapping.

It can cause an ❷_____ , or feeling, of high or low.

The music can be fast or very slow.

The music of Mexico is some of the best.

When I hear a ❸_____ band, I forget the rest!

They wear colorful ❹_____ that brighten the day,

And ❺_____ around at fiestas, they sing and they play.

Then there's ❻_____ , the cowhands' song,

Sung of sadness and joy while they ride along.

Write additional lines to the musical rhyme using the remaining words from the Word List. Share your poetic contribution with the class.

Name_____ Date _____

Music
Terms p. 1

WORD LIST
- patterns
- repetition
- variation
- accented
- beats
- crescendo
- verses
- original
- chorus
- syncopation
- rhythm

Write these words in alphabetical order on a separate sheet of paper. Remember, if more than one word begins with the same letter, look at the second, third, or maybe fourth letter in each word.

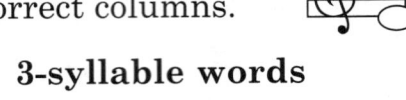

1. Write the words in the correct columns.

   1-syllable word   **3-syllable words**
   _____   _____

   2-syllable words   _____
   _____   _____
   _____   **4-syllable words**
   _____   _____
   _____   _____
   _____   _____
                             _____

2. Write the plural words.
   _____ _____ _____

3. Write the words with a double consonant.
   _____ _____

4. Write the word with the **sh** sound at the beginning of the second syllable.
   _____

TRY THIS — When music builds louder and louder to a climax or a turning point, it is called a *crescendo*. Choose a piece of music that you might enjoy. Listen to it carefully to hear when the crescendo takes place. Brainstorm what other things develop a kind of crescendo and then become peaceful or resolved. Be ready to share your ideas with the class.

 **LET'S READ** — Let's Read these books to see how the plot builds up to a climax, or as in music, a crescendo.
Fool's Gold by Zilpha Keatley Snyder
Low Tide by William Mayne

Name_____ Date _____

Music
Terms p. 2

WORD LIST
- patterns
- repetition
- variation
- accented
- beats
- crescendo
- verses
- original
- chorus
- syncopation
- rhythm

Complete the analogies with words from the Word List.

1. <u>Similarity</u> is to _____ as <u>difference</u> is to _____.

2. <u>Stanzas</u> are to _____ as <u>refrain</u> is to _____.

3. <u>Stressed</u> is to _____ as <u>counts</u> are to _____.

4. <u>Fresh</u> is to _____ as <u>boring</u> is to <u>overdone</u>.

....

Use words from the Word List that fit each of the following clues.

5. Music beginning on an uneven beat _____

6. Music gradually increasing in loudness _____

7. Designs _____

8. The beat of the music _____

....

Write a music review. You may use the same piece of music you used in the *Try This* activity, or you may choose another. You may also use a favorite song. For examples of music reviews, look at magazines or look in the arts section of your Sunday newspaper. Use at least 4 words from the Word List. Share your review with the class.

Extension   Music is universal. Research and write a report about the music of another country. Find out what instruments are commonly used in the music and how the people use music. Find a piece of music that illustrates what you have researched. For example, in Chinese music, the main instruments are the jin and the pipa. If you choose the music of China, you can find out how these instruments are played and if the music has a special purpose.

© Steck-Vaughn Company

Name_____ Date _____

Music
Terms p. 3

WORD LIST
- patterns
- repetition
- variation
- accented
- beats
- crescendo
- verses
- original
- chorus
- syncopation
- rhythm

Complete the passages with words from the Word List.

1. "Jingle Bells, jingle bells,

   Jingle all the way,"

   Is the _____ for a song we sing

   Around a very special wintry day.

   The song has several stanzas, or _____
   if you will.

   They tell about a sleigh ride up and down a snowy hill.

2. Music is made out of _____ of sound.

   In a picture you can see them so you know they're around.

   Patterns can repeat themselves and this is called _____.

   But if a change to the _____ is made,

   it's called a _____.

3. The _____ , or counts, you hear and feel

   Give _____ to the musical creation.

   If uneven beats are _____ , or stressed,

   You have a rhythm called _____.

4. If while listening to some music, it begins to get loud and starts to go fast,

   That's the part called a _____.

   And don't worry, your stereo won't blast!

Name_____ Date_____

Science
Laboratory Equipment p. 1

WORD LIST
- microscope
- beakers
- thermometer
- funnel
- scale
- magnet
- goggles
- mirrors
- corks
- stopwatch
- slides

Write these words in alphabetical order on a separate sheet of paper. Remember, if more than one word begins with the same letter, look at the second, third, or maybe fourth letter in each word.

1. Write the compound word.

   _____

2. Write the words that contain a double consonant.

   _____   _____

   _____

3. Write the words that are plural.

   _____   _____

   _____   _____

4. Write the two-syllable word that contains an **ă** sound and an **ĕ** sound.

   _____

5. Write the word that has 4 syllables.

   _____

6. Write the words that have the **sk** sound.

   _____   _____

 Choose any 5 of the laboratory tools listed in the Word List and tell what each one is used for in an experiment. Then list at least 5 other tools that are used in a laboratory. Illustrate each tool and describe its use.

 Create a poem about the uses of the tools listed in the Word List. Use at least 5 words from the Word List. Share your poem with the class.

Name_____ Date _____

Science
Laboratory Equipment p. 2

Word List
- microscope
- beakers
- thermometer
- funnel
- scale
- magnet
- goggles
- mirrors
- corks
- stopwatch
- slides

Complete the analogies using words from the Word List.

1. <u>Telescope</u> is to <u>astronomy</u> as _____ is to <u>biology</u>.

2. <u>Temperature</u> is to _____ as <u>weight</u> is to _____.

3. <u>Helmet</u> is to <u>head</u> as _____ are to <u>eyes</u>.

4. <u>Tools</u> are to <u>hammers</u> as <u>containers</u> are to _____.

5. <u>Plugs</u> are to <u>sinks</u> as _____ are to <u>bottles</u>.

6. <u>Reflection</u> is to _____ as <u>time</u> is to a _____.

7. <u>Sponge</u> is to <u>water</u> as _____ is to <u>steel</u>.

Match the remaining words from the Word List to these clues.

8. Pieces of glass on which specimens are put _____

9. A piece of equipment for pouring liquid into small-mouthed containers _____

Let's Read these helpful books.
Making and Using Scientific Equipment by David E. Newton
Simple Physics Experiments with Everyday Materials by Judy Breckenridge

Extension Find an experiment that you can easily demonstrate to the class. Gather the materials or tools that you will need. Make a chart showing the steps you will follow. Practice the experiment at home before presenting it to the class. This is a project on which you might want to work with a partner.

Name_____ Date_____

Science
Laboratory Equipment p. 3

Label the pictures with words from the Word List.

WORD LIST
- microscope
- beakers
- thermometer
- funnel
- scale
- magnet
- goggles
- mirrors
- corks
- stopwatch
- slides

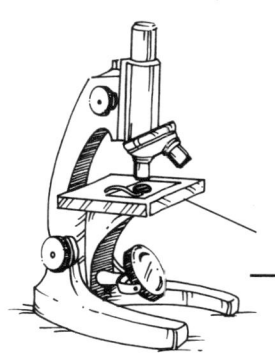

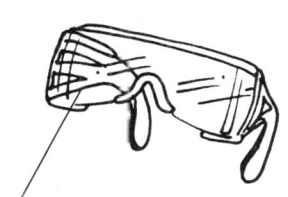
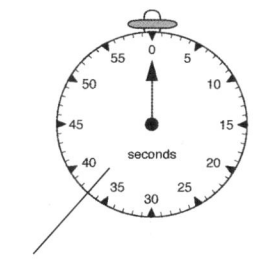

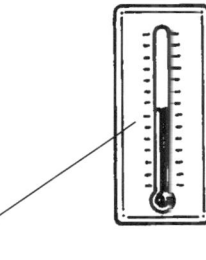

43

Name_____ Date_____

Science
Human Body p. 1

WORD LIST
- tongue
- stomach
- liver
- intestine
- appendix
- swallow
- mouth
- digestion
- esophagus
- saliva
- dissolve

Write these words in alphabetical order on a separate sheet of paper. Remember, if more than one word begins with the same letter, look at the second, third, or maybe fourth letter in each word.

1. Write the words that have a double consonant.

   _____   _____

   _____

2. Write the words that have the ŭ sound in the first syllable.

   _____   _____

3. Write the words in the correct columns.

   1-syllable words   **2-syllable words**

   _____   _____

   _____   _____

   3-syllable words

   _____   _____

   _____   _____

                               4-syllable words

   _____   _____

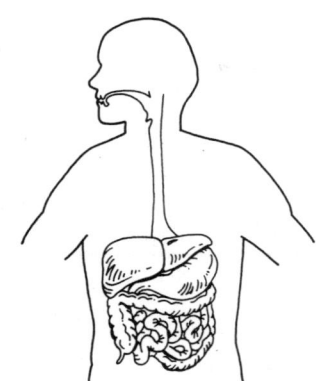

 Research to find the names and purposes of other parts of the digestive system. Then find and write the name of 1 other body system along with its parts and the purpose for each part.

 Imagine you are a carrot that is about to be eaten. From the point of view of the carrot, write what happens in the digestive process. Remember, you are a carrot, not a scientist. Use at least 6 words from the Word List.

© Steck-Vaughn Company   Spelling 6, SV 6747-6

Science
Human Body p. 2

WORD LIST
- tongue
- stomach
- liver
- intestine
- appendix
- swallow
- mouth
- digestion
- esophagus
- saliva
- dissolve

Complete the puzzle with words from the Word List.

Across:
2. Food goes through this to the stomach
4. An upset _____
5. Has lobes
7. Digestion begins here
9. Where food goes from stomach
10. Aids in digestion
11. A non-vital organ

Down:
1. Become liquid, or melt
3. Pass from mouth to stomach
6. Act of changing food in the body
8. Helps us swallow food

Let's Read and "digest" these books.
Search for Delicious by Natalie Babbit
Science Experiments You Can Eat by Vicki Cobb

Extension Using your explanation of the digestive system from the *Let's Write* activity, make charts or illustrations to go with the explanation. Present your project to the class.

Science
Human Body p. 3

WORD LIST
- tongue
- stomach
- liver
- intestine
- appendix
- swallow
- mouth
- digestion
- esophagus
- saliva
- dissolve

Complete the activity introduction, and label the picture with words from the Word List.

The process by which the body changes food so that it can be used to supply energy is called ❶_____.

As you chew, a watery substance known as ❷_____ helps ❸_____ the food. It aids digestion if you chew your food well before you ❹_____.

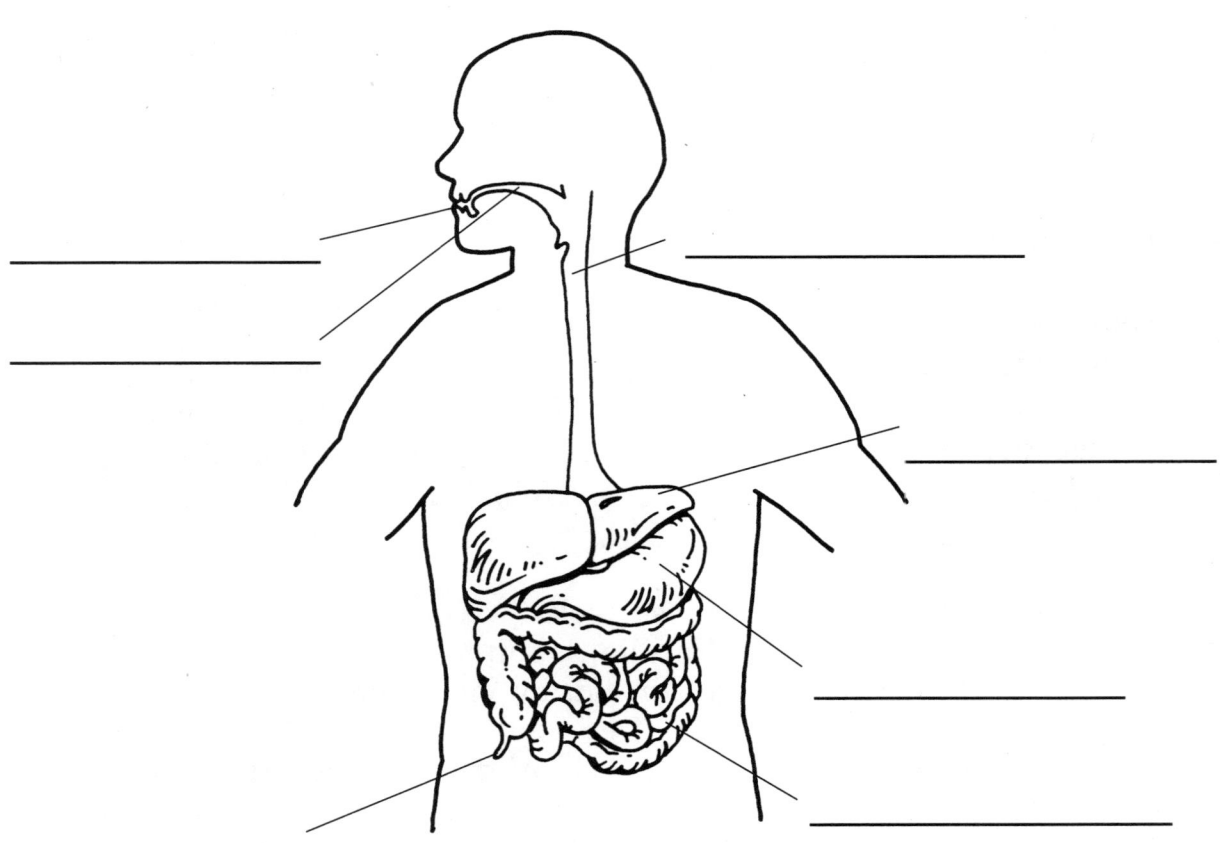

Name_____ Date _____

Science
Technology p. 1

- Internet
- on-line
- browser
- navigate
- communicate
- cyberspace
- download
- bookmarks
- research
- virtual
- sources

Write these words in alphabetical order on a separate sheet of paper. Remember, if more than one word begins with the same letter, look at the second, third, or maybe fourth letter in each word.

1. Write the compound words.

   _____   _____
   _____

2. Write the 3-syllable words.

   _____   _____
   _____

3. Write the words with the **ā** sound in the last syllable.

   _____   _____   _____

4. Write the words that are plural.

   _____   _____

5. Write the words that contain the **ow** sound.

   _____   _____

6. Write the word whose prefix means to *do again*.

   _____

With a partner, brainstorm and list at least 8 other words that come to mind when you think of the Internet. Be sure you are able to give an explanation of the words. As a class, create an Internet dictionary using all the words you have collected as well as the ones from the Word List. In the dictionary, list each word and give the meaning or explanation.

Extension   Research computers. Create a historical time line showing the development of the computer just in the 1990s. Use facts and pictures on the time line. The pictures may be your illustrations or pictures you cut out. Then extend your time line to the year 2005 and show what you think will happen to the computer.

Name_____ Date _____

Science
Technology p. 2

Word List
- Internet
- on-line
- browser
- navigate
- communicate
- cyberspace
- download
- bookmarks
- research
- virtual
- sources

Find the word in the Word List that best fits each clue. Then use the numbered letters to find a synonym for cyberspace and Internet.

1. Navigation program __ __ __ __ __ __ __
                                      14

2. Transfer files to your computer

   __ __ __ __ __ __ __ __
       2   6

3. 2 or more networks connected

   __ __ __ __ __ __ __ __
           4

4. To move around on the Web __ __ __ __ __ __ __ __
                                                   13

5. Allow you to save resource locators

   __ __ __ __ __ __ __ __ __
        5   8

6. Synonym for *Internet*

   __ __ __ __ __ __ __ __ __
    15   10

7. To investigate, or look up __ __ __ __ __ __ __ __
                                                   12

8. To talk back and forth

   __ __ __ __ __ __ __ __ __ __ __
                        7

9. In the flow of things on a computer __ __ - __ __ __ __
                                                     1   11

10. Not real __ __ __ __ __ __ __
                           9

11. Where things come from __ __ __ __ __ __ __
                                     3

Secret word

__ __ f __ __ __ __ __ __ __
1 2   3 4 5 6 7 1 3 2

__ __ __ __ __ __ __ __ __ __
8 9 10 11 4 12 1 13 12 14 6 15

Name_____ Date _____

Science
Technology p. 3

WORD LIST
- Internet
- on-line
- browser
- navigate
- communicate
- cyberspace
- download
- bookmarks
- research
- virtual
- sources

Complete the passage with words from the Word List.

I've got to turn on this computer of mine,

Because what I want is to get ❶_____.

To ❷_____ , read, and get up to speed.

So the help of a Web ❸_____ is what I need.

I liked a browser that I was showed.

But in order to use it, I have to ❹_____.

I transfer the files to my machine,

And am able to ❺_____, or surf, at full steam.

I find several sites that I want to keep handy,

So use what are called ❻_____— they really are dandy!

I'll do ❼_____ for school or browse just for fun.

There are so many ❽_____, it's hard to choose one!

Use the remaining words from the Word List in your own sentences.

LET'S WRITE An acrostic is a poem in which the letters of the first or last words of a line spell a word. Use the word *Internet*. For each letter of the word, write a phrase that describes or tells about the Internet. In the phrases, use at least 4 words from the Word List. Here is an example of an acrostic.

> **F**erris Wheels going 'round and 'round,
> **U**nder the blue sky and hot, hot sun.
> **N**ever-ending good times with someone you like.

Let's Read these "high-tech" books.
Computer Takeover by Edward Packard
Gemini Game by Michael Scott

Name_____ Date_____

Science
Chemistry p. 1

WORD LIST
- matter
- changes
- atoms
- elements
- nucleus
- surrounded
- structure
- compounds
- experiments
- energy
- reactions

Write these words in alphabetical order on a separate sheet of paper. Remember, if more than one word begins with the same letter, look at the second, third, or maybe fourth letter in each word.

1. Write the words that are plural.

   _____ _____
   _____ _____
   _____ _____

2. Write the words that contain a double consonant.

   _____ _____

3. Write the words that begin with a vowel.

   _____ _____
   _____ _____

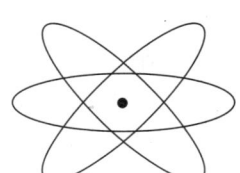

4. Write the words with the **k** sound.

   _____ _____
   _____ _____

 Find and list the names and symbols of at least 5 chemical elements. Find the chemical formulas for water and for salt. Explain what the formulas mean. See if you can find the element that is harmful to a famous super hero who is able to "leap tall buildings."

 Choose at least 5 words from the Word List and write a poem which will help someone understand something about chemistry. For example, you might want to write a poem about an atom.

© Steck-Vaughn Company   Spelling 6, SV 6747-6

Name_____ Date_____

Science
Chemistry p. 2

Word List
- matter
- changes
- atoms
- elements
- nucleus
- surrounded
- structure
- compounds
- experiments
- energy
- reactions

Complete the puzzle with words from the Word List.

Across:
1. Atoms from different elements joined together
4. Tiny particles which make up all elements
7. What happens when acids and bases are mixed
8. What is needed to run, walk, talk
10. Carbon and oxygen are these

Down:
1. Makes different, or alters
2. Central thing
3. Encircled
5. What all things are made of
6. Formation
8. Tests, or trials

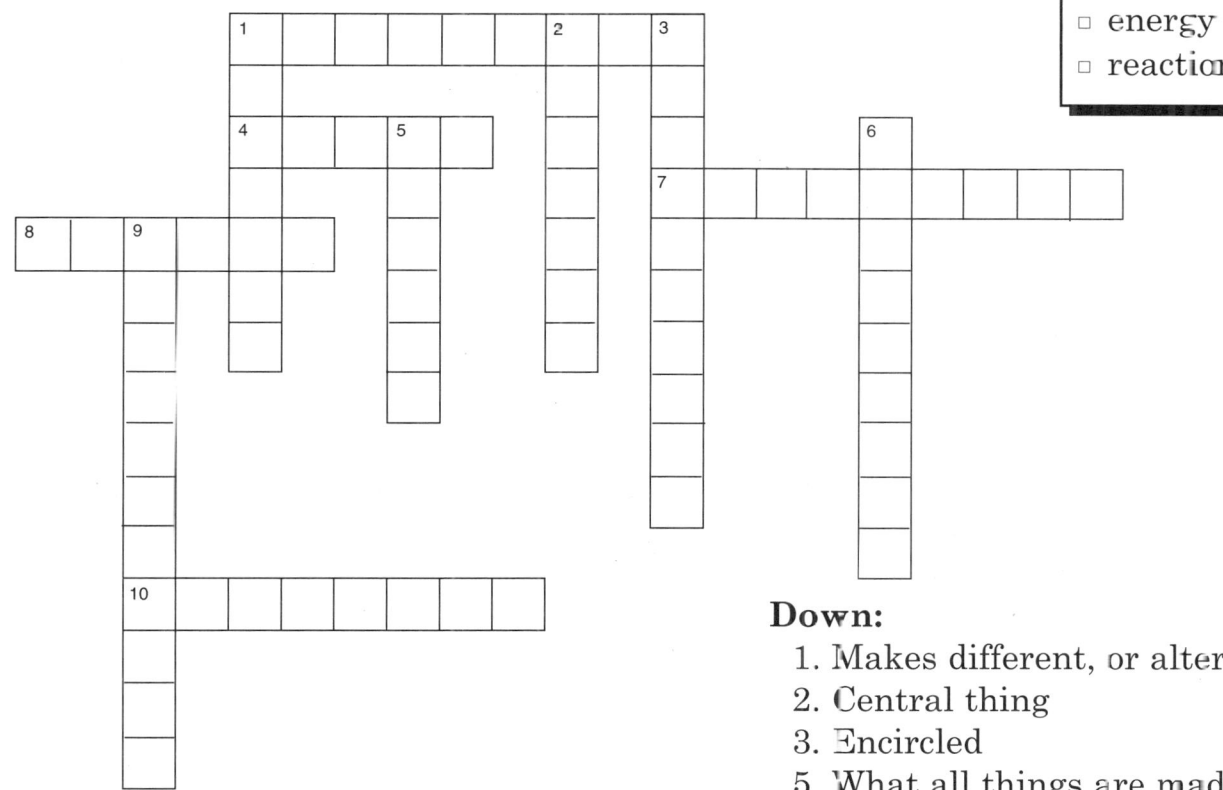

Let's Read these books to see what our "reactions" will be.
Science Projects about Chemistry by Robert Gardner
Chemo Kid by Robert Lipsyte

Extension Make a list of 5 elements that interest you. For each element, research at least 3 facts. Share your information with the class.

Science
Chemistry p. 3

WORD LIST
- matter
- changes
- atoms
- elements
- nucleus
- surrounded
- structure
- compounds
- experiments
- energy
- reactions

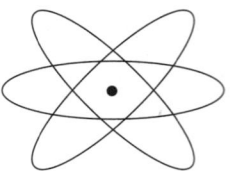

Complete the passage with words from the Word List.

When we study ❶_____, or what all things are made of, we are learning about the science of chemistry. All matter is made up of ❷_____. For example, water is a mixture of the elements hydrogen and oxygen. Among the important scientists who contributed major ideas to advance chemistry is John Dalton. John Dalton developed the theory that all matter is composed of ❸_____. He proved that when the atoms of one element combine with the atoms of another element, they form ❹_____. You can see the ❺_____, or formation, of an atom in the diagram at the top of the page. At the center, or in the middle, of each atom is the ❻_____. The nucleus is ❼_____, or encircled, by electrons. It is important to know that chemical actions, or ❽_____, create ❾_____ in matter's atoms. For example, when the elements iron and oxygen are combined, they form what we know as rust. There are chemical reactions that give off ❿_____, or power. For example, our bodies use chemical reactions to change the food we eat into the energy we need to run and walk. Can you think of any ⓫_____, or tests, showing other chemical reactions and the energy they give off?

Find an experiment, demonstrate it for the class, and explain what is happening.

Name _____ Date _____

Science
Heredity p. 1

WORD LIST
- traits
- chromosomes
- generation
- inherit
- cells
- dominant
- offspring
- cloning
- genes
- recessive
- membrane

Write these words in alphabetical order on a separate sheet of paper. Remember, if more than one word begins with the same letter, look at the second, third, or maybe fourth letter in each word.

1. Write the words that are plural.

   _____   _____
   _____   _____

2. Write the words in the correct column.

   1-syllable words   **2-syllable words**

   _____   _____
   _____   _____
   _____   _____

   3-syllable words   **4-syllable word**

   _____   _____
   _____

A person who studies science is called a scientist. There are specific careers that a person can follow in the field of science. Find and list at least 6 specific careers in science. For each career, identify what each one specializes in and if possible, the name of someone who is associated with that field. Share your findings with the class.

Find out about the "Father of Genetics." After you read about this person, put together a Help Wanted ad for someone who could help him. Use at least 5 words from the Word List. Post your ad on the bulletin board.

Science
Heredity p. 2

Word List
- traits
- chromosomes
- generation
- inherit
- cells
- dominant
- offspring
- cloning
- genes
- recessive
- membrane

Find the word from the Word List that best fits each clue. Then use the numbered letters to find the name of the "Father of Genetics."

1. Thin covering of a cell __ __ __ __ __ __ __ __
    5
2. Occurs in pairs __ __ __ __ __ __ __ __ __ __ __
3. All plants and animals are made of these __ __ __ __ __
                                             8
4. Characteristics __ __ __ __ __ __
                   2
5. Duplicating identical organisms __ __ __ __ __ __ __
6. Prominent, main, major __ __ __ __ __ __ __ __
                          7
7. Units in chromosomes __ __ __ __ __
                        3
8. Group born and living around same time __ __ __ __ __ __ __ __ __ __
                                          1
9. To receive from one another __ __ __ __ __ __ __
                                     6
10. Children __ __ __ __ __ __ __ __ __
              4
11. Being in the background __ __ __ __ __ __ __ __ __

Secret word

__ __ __ __ __ __ __ __ __ __
 1 2 3 1 4 2 5 3 6 7 3 8

Let's Read these books that involve science.
A Bone from a Dry Sea by Peter Dickinson
Nothing but Trouble, Trouble, Trouble by Patricia Hermes

Extension Dolly made the headlines in 1997 when she was cloned. Using library resources and on-line resources, find out who Dolly is and why this made the headlines. Find out what scientists are saying about the purpose and importance of cloning. Share your findings with the class. Report on any other "clones" that scientists have created.

Science
Heredity p. 3

WORD LIST
- traits
- chromosomes
- generation
- inherit
- cells
- dominant
- offspring
- cloning
- genes
- recessive
- membrane

Label the pictures with words from the Word List.

_____   _____

Complete the passage with words from the Word List

Have you ever heard people ask things like, "Did you

❶_____ your blue eyes from you mother?" Maybe your nose looks like your father's nose. Even if you have several ❷_____, or features, that resemble those of your parents, you do not look exactly like either one of them. It is only in a process known as ❸_____ that one organism can be an identical duplicate of another organism. The traits that ❹_____, or children, inherit come from their parents' ❺_____. Half your genes come from your mother and the other half come from your father. Genes that are stronger than other genes are called ❻_____ genes. The weaker genes are called ❼_____ genes. You might even have a trait that comes from your mother's side of the family, which you don't see in your mother. There are genes that skip a ❽_____ and are passed down to the next in line. In other words, you might have a trait that your mother's mother has, but your mother does not have.

Think about traits you share with your parents, grandparents, brothers, or sisters. What traits do you have that you would like to pass on to your own children?

Name_____ Date_____

Science
Astronomy p. 1

WORD LIST
- galaxy
- asteroid
- atmosphere
- sunspot
- nova
- meteor
- telescope
- satellite
- universe
- gravity
- constellation

Write these words in alphabetical order on a separate sheet of paper. Remember, if more than one word begins with the same letter, look at the second, third, or maybe fourth letter in each word.

1. Write the words with a double consonant.
   _____ _____

2. Write the words with 3 syllables.
   _____ _____
   _____ _____
   _____ _____

3. Write the words with 2 syllables.
   _____ _____

 Astronomers have named 88 constellations and approximately 44 can be seen on a clear night. In the ancient world, many constellations were named after gods, heroes, and animals. Research and find the names of 10 constellations and what their names mean. Share your list with the class. See how many different constellations the class can name.

 It is the year 2020. You are trying to sell people the concept of living in space. You need to make living there very appealing. Write a persuasive paragraph. Of course, in order to persuade your readers, your description of what they will see and be able to do must be "out of this world." Use at least 5 words from the Word List.

 Let's Read these "far out" books.
Traveler's Guide to the Solar System by Patricia Barnes-Svaney
Alien Secrets by Annette Curtis Klause

© Steck-Vaughn Company   56   Spelling 6, SV 6747-6

Name _____ Date _____

Science
Astronomy p. 2

WORD LIST
- galaxy
- asteroid
- atmosphere
- sunspot
- nova
- meteor
- telescope
- satellite
- universe
- gravity
- constellation

Find the word in the Word List that best fits each clue. Then use the numbered letters to find the name of 1 of the 12 constellations of the Zodiac.

1. Small, planet-like body that circles the sun
   __ __ __ __ __ __ __ __

2. Layer of gases around a planet
   __ __ __ __ __ __ __ __ __ __

3. Invisible force of attraction between objects
   __ __ __ __ __ __ __
            5

4. Streak of light sometimes seen in night sky
   __ __ __ __ __ __
         4

5. Object in space that orbits a planet
   __ __ __ __ __ __ __ __ __

6. Exploding star __ __ __ __

7. Dark patch on surface of sun __ __ __ __ __ __ __
                                              6

8. Instrument used to view stars
   __ __ __ __ __ __ __ __ __
            3

9. Enormous group of stars, dust, and gases
   __ __ __ __ __ __
      2

10. Stars that form a pattern
    __ __ __ __ __ __ __ __ __ __ __ __ __
    1

11. Earth, the heavens, and the galaxies
    __ __ __ __ __ __ __ __
       7

Secret word

__ __ __ __ __ __ __ __ __
1 2 3 4 5 1 6 4 7

Name_____ Date _____

Science
Astronomy p. 3

WORD LIST
- galaxy
- asteroid
- atmosphere
- sunspot
- nova
- meteor
- telescope
- satellite
- universe
- gravity
- constellation

Label the pictures with words from the Word List.

  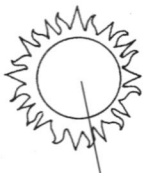 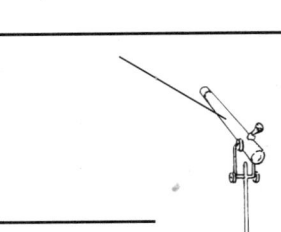

_____ _____ _____ _____

  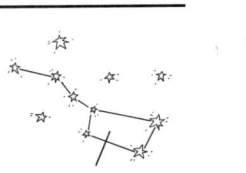

_____ _____ _____

Complete the passage with words from the Word List.

The place we call the ❶_____

Is splendid and mysterious.

Clear, dark skies filled with stars so bright,

You'll even see a ❷_____ on such a night!

Sometimes if the night is right,

I feel that I could take a flight.

I'd give Earth's ❸_____ the slip,

And I'd become my own spaceship.

I'd dip and curve, fly far and near,

While investigating the ❹_____ !

Extension Using the 10 constellations that you found under the *Try This* activity, illustrate the constellations based on what their names mean. For example, if you listed Scorpio as one of your constellations, the name means "scorpion," so you would illustrate a scorpion. You might want to use dark blue or black construction paper and do the diagrams using white ink or chalk. Display the constellations around the classroom.

Name_____ Date _____

Language Arts
Gary Paulsen/*Hatchet* p. 1

WORD LIST
- spasm
- turbulence
- panic
- shelter
- threaten
- survival
- frightened
- spear
- incessant
- frustration
- infuriating

Write these words in alphabetical order on a separate sheet of paper. Remember, if more than one word begins with the same letter, look at the second, third, or maybe fourth letter in each word.

1. Write the words in the correct columns.

1-syllable word   **2-syllable words**
_____   _____

3-syllable words   _____
_____   _____
_____   _____
_____   _____
_____
                          5-syllable words
_____
                          _____

2. Write the words that contain a suffix.

_____   _____
_____   _____
_____   _____

 In the book, *Hatchet*, Brian remembered something Mr. Perpich, his English teacher, had said to the class. He had said, "You are your most valuable asset." Think about this. Write down what you think this means. As a class, share and discuss your thoughts.

 You have interviewed Brian Robeson. He has told you his story of survival during the 54 days he had been stranded in the wilderness. Write a newspaper article based on your interview. Be sure to give the article an interest-grabbing headline. Your article should be at least 3 paragraphs in length. Use at least 7 words from the Word List. Share your article with the class.

Name_____ Date_____

Language Arts
Gary Paulsen/*Hatchet* p. 2

WORD LIST
- spasm
- turbulence
- panic
- shelter
- threaten
- survival
- frightened
- spear
- incessant
- frustration
- infuriating

Complete the puzzle with words from the Word List.

Across:
2. Discouragement
4. Extreme fear
6. Housing
8. Sudden movement of muscle
9. Making one angry
10. A knife-like weapon

Down:
1. Violent motion
3. Continuous
5. Scared
6. Staying alive
7. To make threats

Let's Read these other books by Gary Paulsen.
Tracker
Dogsong

Extension Do an author study on Gary Paulsen. Write a short biography. Include the number of books he has written and how many of them have won awards. Include a time line showing when each of his books was published. Then, read 1 of the other books and try to "sell" it to the class.

Name_____ Date _____

Language Arts
Gary Paulsen/*Hatchet* p. 3

WORD LIST
- spasm
- turbulence
- panic
- shelter
- threaten
- survival
- frightened
- spear
- incessant
- frustration
- infuriating

Complete the passage with words from the Word List.

The guide led us into the cavern. We were finally on our way! Nothing more could ❶_____ our progress. We had waited three days to get started. Each time we thought we had the go-ahead, something else would happen. Our ❷_____ and anger were beginning to show. Three of us had had to train hard to get in shape for this excursion. We had worked so hard that our muscles would ❸_____ from exertion. We also had taken a course in ❹_____ skills. The main thing the instructor said was, "Don't ❺_____!" We were told to remain calm and think about what we had learned. We learned we should look for ❻_____, or covering, first. We even learned how to make a ❼_____ using a stick and a knife. We reviewed everything we had learned as we flew to the starting point of our trip. We thought we might need our survival skills right away as we experienced some ❽_____ on the small plane. It felt like we were in a wind tunnel. Indeed, we had been ❾_____! Once we landed, we were told to stay put. There was a severe storm approaching. At first it was ❿_____. We were angry! On the second day of waiting, we became depressed. Were we ever going to start? The rain was constant. At night we listened to its ⓫_____ pounding. It didn't let up for two days. On the third day, we were rewarded. The rain eased up, and the sun even made an appearance. We were told we could start out the next day. And so, we were on our way. Surely, nothing else would happen.

What do you think? Did the people in the story complete the excursion? On a separate sheet of paper, write what you think happened.

Name_____ Date_____

Language Arts
Paragraphs p. 1

WORD LIST
- chronological
- contrast
- arrange
- comparison
- importance
- details
- accurate
- emphasize
- summarize
- narrative
- descriptive

Write these words in alphabetical order on a separate sheet of paper. Remember, if more than one word begins with the same letter, look at the second, third, or maybe fourth letter in each word.

1. Write the words that end with suffix **-tive**.
   _____   _____

2. Write the words that end with the suffix **-ize**.
   _____   _____

3. Write the words that end with the suffixes **-al** or **-ance**.
   _____   _____

4. Write the words that contain a double consonant.
   _____   _____
   _____   _____

1940

5. Write the 2-syllable words.
   _____   _____
   _____

1920

6. Write the 4-syllable word.
   _____

There are 2 other kinds of paragraphs besides the 2 in the Word List. List the names of all 4 types of paragraphs. Describe the significance for each kind. Find an example for each. You may use any resources, such as newspapers, magazines, textbooks, or novels.

Write a paragraph telling how you would go about writing a descriptive or a narrative paragraph. Use at least 5 words from the Word List. Share your paragraph with the class.

Name_____ Date _____

Language Arts
Paragraphs p. 2

WORD LIST
- chronological
- contrast
- arrange
- comparison
- importance
- details
- accurate
- emphasize
- summarize
- narrative
- descriptive

Complete the analogies with words from the Word List.

1. Balance is to symmetrical as order is to _____.

2. Lengthen is to expand as condense is to _____.

3. Similarity is to _____ as difference is to contradiction.

4. Incorrect is to faulty as correct is to _____.

5. Scatter is to disturb as organize is to _____.

6. Significance is to _____ as frailty is to weakness.

Write the remaining words from the Word List that best fit each clue.

7. Paragraph that gives details of an experience _____

8. To highlight an event _____

9. Facts that support a main idea _____

10. Paragraph that gives a clear picture of a person, place, or thing _____

11. To find differences between things _____

 Let's Read these books.
Playing Beatie Bow by Ruth Park
Alexandra by Scott O'Dell

Extension   In the 1950s, Charles Schulz produced the *Peanuts* comic strip. In 1952, *Charlotte's Web* was published. In 1955, *The Cat in the Hat* was written by Dr. Seuss. Choose 1 of the events. Find out more about the titles and/or writers. Write a report. Your report should include at least 1 descriptive paragraph and 1 narrative paragraph. Share your report with the class.

Language Arts
Paragraphs p. 3

WORD LIST
- chronological
- contrast
- arrange
- comparison
- importance
- details
- accurate
- emphasize
- summarize
- narrative
- descriptive

Complete the passage with words from the Word List.

A paragraph focuses on one topic with supporting ❶_____ to give a reader an interesting picture of the topic. If the paragraph talks about and gives a clear picture of a single person, place, or thing, it is called a ❷_____ paragraph. If the paragraph gives the details of an event in story form, it is called a ❸_____ . Usually, the writer will ❹_____ , or organize, the events in the order in which they happened, or in ❺_____ order. In some paragraphs, the writer will arrange the events in order of ❻_____ . This arrangement can be from the most important to the least, or vice versa. If a writer wants to explain a subject by showing how it is similar to another, this is called ❼_____ . On the other hand, if the writer wants to show the differences between two subjects, this is called ❽_____ . In an expository paragraph, the writer should make sure that all facts or directions are ❾_____ , or correct. You cannot ❿_____ , or stress, enough the importance of accuracy. Lastly, some paragraphs express an opinion, and try to convince the reader to accept the opinion. Now to ⓫_____ , or review, what has been said about paragraphs. A paragraph can describe, tell a story, explain something, or express an opinion. Whatever kind of paragraph you write, make the details support the main idea. Have fun writing!

Name_____ Date_____

Language Arts
Kinds of Literature p. 1

WORD LIST
- mythology
- poetry
- imagery
- biography
- imagination
- significant
- prose
- belief
- vivid
- adaptation
- phenomenon

Write these words in alphabetical order on a separate sheet of paper. Remember, if more than one word begins with the same letter, look at the second, third, or maybe fourth letter in each word.

1. Write the words in which the letter **y** has the **ē** sound.

   _____ _____
   _____ _____

2. Write the word in which the letter **y** has the **ĭ** sound.

   _____

3. Write the words that have 2 syllables.

   _____ _____

4. Write the words that have the suffix **-tion**.

   _____ _____

5. Write the words that contain the **f** sound.

   _____ _____
   _____ _____

6. Write the 1-syllable word.

   _____

 There are 3 literature genres in the Word List. They are poetry, mythology, and biography. Brainstorm and list at least 5 other genres. List the title of 1 selection for each genre, including the 3 in the Word List. Share your list and examples with the class.

 Choose 1 of the selections you mentioned under the *Try This* activity. Read the selection. Write a critical review of the selection. Use at least 5 words from the Word List in the review. For examples of reviews, look in the book or arts section of the newspaper. Share your review with the class.

Name_____ Date_____

Language Arts
Kinds of Literature p. 2

WORD LIST
- mythology
- poetry
- imagery
- biography
- imagination
- significant
- prose
- belief
- vivid
- adaptation
- phenomenon

Complete the analogies with words from the Word List.

1. <u>Dark</u> is to <u>dull</u> as <u>bright</u> is to _____ .

2. <u>Fact</u> is to <u>opinion</u> as <u>doubt</u> is to _____ .

3. <u>Minor</u> is to <u>unimportant</u> as <u>major</u> is to _____ .

4. <u>Concrete</u> is to <u>reality</u> as <u>allusion</u> is to _____ .

5. <u>Haiku</u> is to _____ as <u>novel</u> is to _____ .

Complete the puzzle with the remaining words from the Word List.

Across:
2. Folklore, legends
4. Change
5. A rare occurrence

Down:
1. Mental pictures
3. Account of a person's life written by another

Let's Read these books.
Joyful Noise: Poems for Two Voices by Paul Fleischman
Why the Sun and the Moon Live in the Sky by Elphinstone Dayrell

Extension Mythology consists of stories that people have told one another over the years. Later, these stories were written down. Myths are stories about heroes or gods or stories that try to explain "why" something has happened in our world. For example, have you ever wondered why giraffes have such long necks? Create a myth that explains the "why" of something. Share your story with the class. Publish a class book of "why" stories.

© Steck-Vaughn Company 66 Spelling 6, SV 6747-6

Name_____ Date_____

Language Arts
Kinds of Literature p. 3

WORD LIST
- mythology
- poetry
- imagery
- biography
- imagination
- significant
- prose
- belief
- vivid
- adaptation
- phenomenon

Complete the passages with words from the Word List.

1. Why does a raccoon have a mask? Why does a skunk have a white stripe down its back? Or, for that matter, how did the animals get their names? Why is a lion called a lion and not an elephant? Sit back, relax, and let your ❶_____ go wild. Let your mind paint mental pictures about the why and how. Your mental pictures can be as ❷_____, or as colorful, as you want them to be. The study of myths is called ❸_____. Myths, legends, and folktales are known as folklore. Myths were begun to explain a ❹_____ that a group of people had in something. These stories were told orally and passed down from one generation to another. Myths could also explain a strange occurrence, or ❺_____, before people had the scientific knowledge to explain such events. A written version of one of these tales is an ❻_____ of the oral version. Through the years, bits and pieces were added to these stories to make them even more spectacular.

2. Have you ever read a story about someone's life that wasn't written by that person? If you have, you have read a ❶_____. In a biography, the writer tries to write about the ❷_____, or important, events in a person's life. A biography is considered a piece of ❸_____. This is in contrast to ❹_____ in which a writer uses much ❺_____, like similes and metaphors, and often writes in verse.

Name_____ Date _____

Language Arts
Research Paper p. 1

WORD LIST
- thesis
- statement
- outline
- documentation
- revise
- grammar
- mechanics
- credit
- experts
- periodicals
- clarity

Write these words in alphabetical order on a separate sheet of paper. Remember, if more than one word begins with the same letter, look at the second, third, or maybe fourth letter in each word.

1. Write the words that are plural.

   _____ _____
   _____

2. Write the words with 2 syllables.

   _____ _____ _____
   _____ _____

3. Write the words with 5 syllables. Write the base words.

   _____ _____
   _____ _____

4. Write the word that ends with the ē sound.

   _____

Brainstorm and list at least 6 topics that interest you. Use a variety of sources to find ideas. You can use books, magazines, computer, encyclopedias, newspapers, or television. Arrange the list in the order of your interest. Take your first choice and make a web. Write your topic in the center of the web. Draw lines from the main topic and for each line, write down things you would like to read and learn about this topic. Here is an example for the topic *weather*:

```
    seasonal ── WEATHER ── disasters
                 │    │
     how it affects   meteorologists
        people
```

Name_____ Date_____

Language Arts
Research Paper p. 2

Word List
- thesis
- statement
- outline
- documentation
- revise
- grammar
- mechanics
- credit
- experts
- periodicals
- clarity

Complete the analogies with words from the Word List.

1. <u>Amateurs</u> are to <u>novices</u> as <u>professionals</u> are to _____.

2. <u>Inaccuracy</u> is to <u>confusion</u> as <u>accuracy</u> is to _____.

3. <u>Copying</u> is to <u>plagiarism</u> as <u>proof</u> is to _____.

Write the word from the Word List that best fits each clue.

4. Journals, magazines, pamphlets   _____
5. Recognition   _____
6. Proposal   _____
7. A plan   _____
8. System of rules for writing   _____
9. Technical aspects of writing   _____
10. Edit or change   _____
11. An assertion or declaration   _____

 You have done 1 of the first steps in producing a research paper in the Try This activity. Think about what you have to do next. Using at least 6 words from the Word List, write the steps you should take to have a completed report. Share the steps with the class.

 Let's Read these books that might give you some research ideas.
Living in Space by Larry Kettlekamp
The Vanishing Wetlands by Trent Duffy

Extension   Follow the steps you set up under the *Let's Write* activity. Now is the time to get started on your research project. Do everything up to and including making an outline. Once you have your outline, check to see if your teacher wants you to continue. Be sure to take notes and document your information. Good luck!

Name_____ Date _____

Language Arts
Research Paper p. 3

WORD LIST
- thesis
- statement
- outline
- documentation
- revise
- grammar
- mechanics
- credit
- experts
- periodicals
- clarity

Label the following with words from the word list.

```
I._____
  A._____
    1._____
    2._____
II._____
```

_____

_____

Complete the passage with words from the Word List.

Get ready! Get set! Go! You are now on the course to writing a research paper. Did you gather as many resources as you could? Don't forget the ❶_____, or the people who know more about your topic than anybody else. For example, if your report is on medicine, you might want to interview a doctor. Make sure you make note cards of the resources you use so you can give ❷_____ to the authors of those materials. This ❸_____ is important, especially if you need to prove something. Your resources and documentation will be listed in a bibliography. As you use the resources, take notes. Be sure to copy direct quotes from a resource correctly.

You are on the right track. You have notes. Now, you should write a ❹_____, or proposal. This proposal is a ❺_____ explaining what your main idea is and could list reasons that support your main idea. The thesis should have ❻_____ . Accuracy in your thesis statement will help guide you. You can now make an outline for the rest of the paper. Your outline will be the blueprint for how you want to build your paper.

Now you are ready to write a first draft. When it is completed, you will go back and ❼_____ , or edit, the paper. At this time you will check to make sure you are following the ❽_____ , or rules, for writing. These rules include all the rules of ❾_____ , including spelling and punctuation. Write your final draft. Choose a title that will interest others in your paper.

© Steck-Vaughn Company

Name_____ Date_____

Language Arts
Journal Writing p. 1

WORD LIST
- personal
- respond
- travel
- log
- daily
- experiences
- dialogue
- observations
- reflection
- memories
- diary

Write these words in alphabetical order on a separate sheet of paper. Remember, if more than one word begins with the same letter, look at the second, third, or maybe fourth letter in each word.

1. Write the words that are plural.

   _____   _____

   _____

2. Write the words that end with the ē sound.

   _____   _____

3. Write the words with 3 syllables.

   _____   _____

   _____   _____

   _____

4. Write the 1-syllable word.

   _____

5. Write the 2-syllable words.

   _____   _____   _____

Start keeping a journal. All you need is a notebook, a pen or pencil, and quiet time to write. You should try to write every day. Right now, think about how your day has been going. Take a few minutes and write down your thoughts. For example, if you passed a test, you might be feeling great. However, if you failed the test, you might feel just the opposite. Or, write about some event that you are looking forward to or are concerned about. Try to take at least 5 minutes every day to write in your journal.

Let's Read these books that might encourage you to write.
Dear Mr. Henshaw by Beverly Cleary
Harriet the Spy by Louise Fitzhugh
My Side of the Mountain by Jean George

Name_____ Date_____

Language Arts
Journal Writing p. 2

WORD LIST
- personal
- respond
- travel
- log
- daily
- experiences
- dialogue
- observations
- reflection
- memories
- diary

Complete the analogies with words from the Word List.

1. General is to public as private is to _____.
2. Solo is to duet as monologue is to _____.
3. Annual is to yearly as everyday is to _____.
4. Speak is to talk as answer is to _____.
5. Events are to _____ as remembrances are to _____.

Complete the puzzle with the remaining words from the Word List.

Across:
2. Things noticed
4. Daily personal record
5. Record of travel

Down:
1. Thought
3. To go places

**Extension** Did you know you can have a journal for just about anything? How about a Travel Log? You can do this without even leaving home. Think about places you would like to visit. Find 5 places that you would like to see. Write down the name of each place, where it is located, and at least 4 facts about the place that are reasons for your wanting to visit. Share your "vacation spots" with the class.

LET'S WRITE You can use different types of writing in your journal. On some days, you might just feel like writing simple sentences. However, on other days, you might feel a little more poetic. Write a poem about journal writing. For example:

Writing down one's memories is very personal.
Reflections can be humorous or inspirational.

Use at least 5 words from the Word List.

Name_____ Date _____

Language Arts
Journal Writing p. 3

WORD LIST
- personal
- respond
- travel
- log
- daily
- experiences
- dialogue
- observations
- reflection
- memories
- diary

Complete the passage with words from the Word List.

Sept. 4

Three of us went to Great America today. You wouldn't believe one of the ❶ _____ we had while waiting in line for a ride! Two kids a lot bigger than us try to get in front of us. We lucked out, though. A security person was just walking by. This experience brought back ❷ _____ of what happened to me 2 years ago. I would like to forget them!

Sept. 5

This journal writing is fun. I don't know about doing it ❸ _____ . Every day seems to be a lot. I don't think I want to share this with anyone, either. After all, I might say something ❹ _____ that I don't want anyone else to know. This is the first time I have kept a ❺ _____ . I thought all diaries had locks on them! Mr. Garcia told us this is a different kind of journal. If we want, we can write back and forth to each other. We can write about something and he will read it and ❻ _____ to it. He calls it a ❼ _____ journal because we talk to each other.

Sept. 6

Here goes! Mr. Garcia suggested that we write down our ❽ _____ , or our thoughts, about yesterday's speaker. She wasn't very interesting. I started to fall asleep! But she did say some things that I thought were important. She said that we have to think for ourselves. We shouldn't let anyone pressure us into doing something we don't want to do. She's right. I've got to think for myself!
(This is a good ❾ _____ on what was said. See, even though you almost fell asleep, you learned something. Keep up the good work! Mr. Garcia)

Sept. 7

Write an entry using the remaining 2 words from Word List.

© Steck-Vaughn Company   Spelling 6 SV 6747-6

Language Arts
Media p. 1

WORD LIST
- libel
- slant
- stereotype
- format
- circulation
- anchor
- advertising
- bias
- propaganda
- commercial
- media

Write these words in alphabetical order on a separate sheet of paper. Remember, if more than one word begins with the same letter, look at the second, third, or maybe fourth letter in each word.

1. Write the 4-syllable words.

   _____ _____

   _____ _____

2. Write the 2-syllable words.

   _____ _____

   _____ _____

3. Write the 3-syllable words.

   _____ _____

4. Write the 1-syllable word.

   _____

5. Write the word that contains a silent letter.

   _____

 For one day, keep track of the commercials you see on television or hear on the radio. Keep track of the number of times you see or hear each commercial. Be ready to share the information with the class. Choose your favorite commercial and explain what it is "selling" and why it is your favorite.

Let's Write Write a report on what you think of the use of advertising and commercials. Talk about both the pros and cons. Try to use specific examples of ads or commercials to make your points. Use at least 6 words from the Word List. Share the report with the class.

Name_____ Date_____

Language Arts
Media p. 2

WORD LIST
- libel
- slant
- stereotype
- format
- circulation
- anchor
- advertising
- bias
- propaganda
- commercial
- media

Write the word from the Word List that best fits each clue.

1. Host of a news program _____

2. Means of mass communication _____

3. Arrangement of scheduling _____

4. Point of view _____

5. Number of copies sold _____

6. Calling public attention to the qualities of something _____

7. Spoken or written statement injuring a person's reputation _____

8. Prejudice _____

9. Widespread promotion of ideas _____

10. A paid advertisement on radio or TV _____

11. A fixed notion about something _____

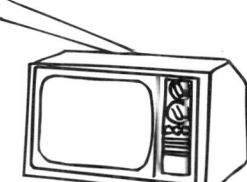

 Let's Read these books and see if you can "sell" them to your classmates.
Darnell Rock Reporting by Walter Dean Meyers
Callender Papers by C. Voigt

Extension Keep a media journal for 1 week. In the journal, keep track of how much time you spend watching television, listening to the radio, reading newspapers, magazines and books, and going to the movies each day. Compare your journal with the others in the class. You will be amazed at how much time you spend involved with the media.

Language Arts
Media p.3

Word List
- libel
- slant
- stereotype
- format
- circulation
- anchor
- advertising
- bias
- propaganda
- commercial
- media

Complete the passage with words from the Word List.

The ❶ _____ of television brings news and entertainment into your home. If you turn on your TV at 5:00 in the evening, here is the ❷ _____ of the show. For the first 10 minutes or so, you will watch a local ❸ _____ person give the latest news from around your city or state. Just as you are getting into the news, there will be a break for a ❹ _____ . Of course, the company who is ❺ _____ this commercial pays a lot of money to have that spot for its ad. But a company advertising on television does not have to worry as much about ❻ _____ , like in newspapers or magazines. The ❼ _____ , or point of view, of the commercial is always that the product or service advertised is the best, and you can't do without it. This is ❽ _____ , the widespread promotion of ideas. You know of course that there is a large degree of ❾ _____ , or prejudice, in commercials. You usually hear only what is good or positive about the product or service. Sometimes advertisers ❿ _____ , or typecast who the buyer or user of a product will be. Do you know of any commercials or ads whose writers are guilty of stereotyping? You don't find too many occasions in advertising in which companies are accused of ⓫ _____ , however. Companies are very careful not to ruin another person's or another company's reputation.

If you can, tape a half-hour television show. If you do not have a TV or a VCR, work with a partner. See if you can determine how much time is devoted to the actual show and how much time is devoted to commercials.

Name_____ Date _____

Math
Probability/Statistics p. 1

WORD LIST
- probability
- mean
- mode
- range
- median
- frequency
- outcomes
- favorable
- diagrams
- surveyed
- chance

Write these words in alphabetical order on a separate sheet of paper. Remember, if more than one word begins with the same letter, look at the second, third, or maybe fourth letter in each word.

1. Write the words that have the $\bar{e}$ sound in the first syllable.

   _____ _____

   _____

2. Write the words that are plural.

   _____ _____

3. Write the words that have the $\bar{a}$ sound in the first syllable.

   _____ _____

4. Write the word that has 5 syllables.

   _____

5. Write the 1 syllable words.

   _____ _____

   _____ _____

6. Write the word that is the past tense.

   _____

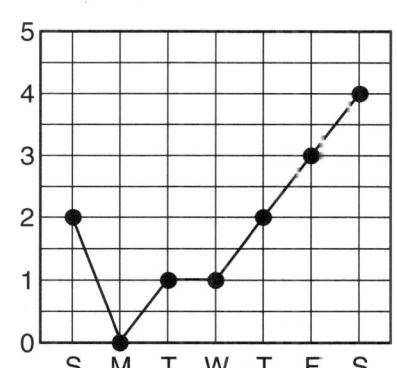

 Choose a topic on which to survey the class. Suggestions include favorite sports teams, favorite movie during the current month, favorite Monday night TV show, favorite board game, or favorite subject. You may choose any other topic you find interesting. Calculate and chart your results and present them to the class.

 Write a math problem in which you want the others to find the relative frequency for something happening. For example: 5 out of 10 people at the local health club use the treadmill for exercise. If during the day 200 people come in, how many people will use the treadmill? (Answer is 100 people.) Use at least 4 words from the Word List. Share your problems.

© Steck-Vaughn Company

Name_____ Date _____

Math
Probability/Statistics p. 2

WORD LIST
- probability
- mean
- mode
- range
- median
- frequency
- outcomes
- favorable
- diagrams
- surveyed
- chance

Write the word from the Word List that best fits each clue.

1. Helpful, agreeable _____

2. Probability of something happening _____

3. A study of the likelihood that something will happen _____

4. Sum of numbers divided by number of addends _____

5. Score or number found most frequently in a set _____

6. The middle number in a set _____

7. Number of times something occurs _____

8. Charts _____

9. Polled or asked _____

10. Possible results in a probability experiment _____

11. Difference between the greatest and the least possibility _____

Let's Read these books.
What Do You Mean by "Average"? by Elizabeth James and Carol Barkin
Do You Wanna Bet? by Jean Cushman

Extension Mathematics is an integral part of our everyday lives. Remember, math is more than just numbers. Keep a math journal and write down each time you use something related to math. For example, if you listen to the weather forecast, you hear the temperature in terms of degrees. At the end of the experiment, compare results with the class. Find out how many different uses for math have been logged.

Name_____ Date_____

Math
Probability/Statistics p. 3

WORD LIST
- probability
- mean
- mode
- range
- median
- frequency
- outcomes
- favorable
- diagrams
- surveyed
- chance

1. The formula for finding out the relative _____, how often or how many times, of _____, or effects, is called the ratio. This is how the formula works:

$$\frac{\text{frequency of the outcome}}{\text{total frequencies of outcomes}}$$

This illustration is one example of what we call _____, or charts, because it shows a plan for how to go about figuring something out.

2. The study of _____, or the likelihood that something will take place, can be interesting, fun, and important. For example, during election time, people who work in campaigns rely on this. After workers have _____, or gotten information from, a number of voters, the workers will tally the results to find out what the most _____, or agreeable, item was. Based on that, the workers will make a prediction that if certain actions are taken, their candidate will get the vote. Is this totally reliable? No, but at least it gives the campaign workers something to work with. Often times, campaign managers will take the _____ that the result of the survey will help their candidate do better in the election. Statisticians will usually look at the _____, or average, age of those being surveyed. Then, they will find the _____, or middle, age group. The age group that appears most frequently is the _____ . The _____ of ages is the difference between the oldest and the youngest. All of these things are important factors for campaign managers to know. This way, they can help guide their candidate to victory.

Math
Graphs p. 1

Word List
- vertical
- horizontal
- axes
- quadrants
- plane
- data
- collecting
- prediction
- reporting
- coordinates
- origin

Write these words in alphabetical order on a separate sheet of paper. Remember, if more than one word begins with the same letter, look at the second, third, or maybe fourth letter in each word.

1. Write the words that contain the **ā** sound.
   _____   _____

2. Write the plural words.
   _____   _____

3. Write the words that have 4 syllables.
   _____   _____

4. Write the words that have 3 syllables.
   _____   _____
   _____

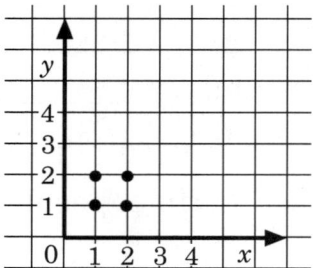

 Get ready to do some graphing! First, find out about the different kinds of graphs, including the circle, bar, line, double bar, and double line graphs. Second, identify what information each graph illustrates. Save this information. You'll be using it later.

 You found out in *Try This* about the different kinds of graphs and their uses. Now, create a line graph. First of all, collect the high temperatures for one week. Second, create the graph. Third, write an explanation describing how you went about constructing the graph. Use at least 6 words from the Word List in your explanation.

Name _____   Date _____

Math
Graphs p. 2

WORD LIST
- vertical
- horizontal
- axes
- quadrants
- plane
- data
- collecting
- prediction
- reporting
- coordinates
- origin

Complete the puzzle with words from the Word List.

Across:
2. Flat surface extending endlessly in all directions
4. Pair of numbers giving location of a point
6. Up and down
9. A guess as to what might happen based on information
11. Gathering

Down:
1. An east to west line
3. Plural form of axis
5. 4 sections created by the coordinate axes
7. Information
8. Telling
10. Beginning point

Let's Read these books that will help you think mathematically.
The Turtle Street Trading Co. by Jill Ross Klevin
Jason and the Money Tree by Sonia Levitin

Extension Find examples of the different kinds of graphs. Look in reference books, textbooks, magazines, and newspapers. Put each graph on a separate sheet of construction paper. Write down what information each graph illustrates. Choose one graph to make a presentation to the class.

Math
Graphs p. 3

WORD LIST
- vertical
- horizontal
- axes
- quadrants
- plane
- data
- collecting
- prediction
- reporting
- coordinates
- origin

Complete the sentences with words from the Word List. Refer to the graph.

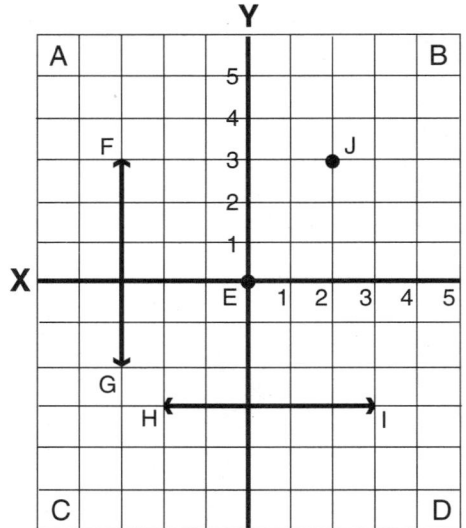

1. A, B, C, and D are _____ .

2. FG is a _____ line.

3. HI is a _____ line.

4. X and Y are the _____ on this graph.

5. E is the _____ on this graph.

6. X-2, and Y-3 are the _____ for J.

Complete the passage with words from the Word List.

A graph is a clear visual way of ❼_____ , or giving, ❽_____ , or information. Before reporting, you must go about ❾_____ , or gathering, all of the data. Then study the facts. Think about how you can best chart or graph the data. Once you have the information charted, see if you can make a ❿_____ , or a guess, as to what might occur if things continue happening in the same way.

One word from the Word List has not been used on this page. Find the different meanings for this word and write a sentence that identifies how it would be used in this context.

Name_____ Date_____

Math
Pre-Algebra p. 1

WORD LIST
- expression
- binomial
- coefficient
- exponent
- operations
- factors
- base
- calculate
- expanded
- associative
- commutative

Write these words in alphabetical order on a separate sheet of paper. Remember, if more than one word begins with the same letter, look at the second, third, or maybe fourth letter in each word.

1. Write the words that end with the suffix **-tive**.

   _____   _____

2. Write the words in the correct columns.

   1-syllable word   **2-syllable word**

   _____   _____

   3-syllable words   **4-syllable words**

   _____   _____

   _____   _____

   _____   _____

3^5

3. Write the words that contain a double consonant.

   _____   _____

   _____   _____

TRY THIS Have you ever though about the practicality of studying Algebra? You are on a debate team. You are on the side in which you have to defend, or state the positives, of studying this area of Math. Write a winning argument. Present your argument to the class.

LET'S WRITE Rap music is chanting in rhythm and rhyme. Make up a rap song about Algebra. Use at least 5 words from the Word List. You could say, for example, "If the base is 3 and the exponent is 3, you have an expression read 3 factors of 3." The chants should make sense. This might be a fun way to learn the meaning of algebraic terms.

Name_____ Date_____

Math
Pre-Algebra p. 2

WORD LIST
- expression
- binomial
- coefficient
- exponent
- operations
- factors
- base
- calculate
- expanded
- associative
- commutative

Write the word from the Word List that best fits each clue.

1. Numbers connected to each other by multiplication _____

2. An equation _____

3. Number part of term like 8y _____

4. Order in which numbers are added or multiplied does not change the answer _____

5. Way in which 3 numbers are grouped with ( ) in which addition or multiplication does not change the answer _____

6. A small raised number showing how many times a number is used as a factor in multiplication _____

7. Method of writing a numeral to show the value of each digit _____

8. 2 terms joined by a plus or minus sign _____

9. Number that is raised to a power _____

10. Addition, division, subtraction _____

11. To estimate or determine answer _____

Let's Read these "problem solving" books. Algebra won't help you solve these problems.
Just a Little Ham by Joan Carris
There's No Surf in Cleveland by Stephanie Jona Buehler

Name_____ Date_____

Math
Pre-Algebra p. 3

WORD LIST
- expression
- binomial
- coefficient
- exponent
- operations
- factors
- base
- calculate
- expanded
- associative
- commutative

Label the following with words from the Word List.

3^5

a. _____
b. _____

$3 + 2 = 2 + 3$ $3X$

c. _____   d. _____

$(3 + 2) + 4 = 3 + (2 + 4)$ $(x - y)$

e. _____   f. _____

$2 \times 7 = 14$ $3{,}426 = 3$ thousands, 4 hundreds, 2 tens, 6 ones

g. _____   h. _____ notation

Complete the following passage with words from the Words List.

In using any of the ❶ _____ , like addition, subtraction, division, or multiplication, you must ❷ _____ , or estimate, the answer. Math is made up of so many parts. It is a combination of numbers, operations, variables, or parentheses. Each group is called an ❸ _____ .

Extension Choose and research a famous mathematician. Tell something about how the person became interested in math and what contribution he or she made to the field. Then write a letter to this person telling what you think about the contribution. Share your findings and letter with the class.

Name_____ Date _____

Math
Geometry p. 1

WORD LIST
- congruent
- figure
- corresponding
- segment
- angle
- polygons
- regular
- diagonal
- rhombus
- vertex
- hypotenuse

Write these words in alphabetical order on a separate sheet of paper. Remember, if more than one word begins with the same letter, look at the second, third, or maybe fourth letter in each word.

1. Write the words in the correct columns.

   2-syllable words   **3-syllable words**
   _____   _____
   _____   _____
   _____   _____
   _____
   _____

   4-syllable words
   _____
   _____
   _____

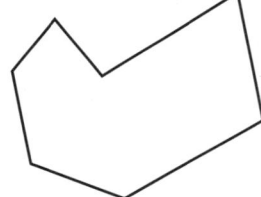

2. Write the word that contains a silent **h**.

   _____

 Polygons are formed by enclosing an area with straight lines. Think about this description of polygons. Look through magazines and cut out pictures that contain polygons or that are polygons. Make a collage of the pictures. Outline the polygons with a black marker.

 Choose a polygon to draw. Inside the shape of the polygon, write a poem about it. Use at least 5 words from the Word List in the poem. Remember, a poem does not need to rhyme. Look up different kinds of poems to help you get started. Share your poem with the class.

Name_____ Date_____

Math
Geometry p. 2

Complete the puzzle with words from the Word List.

WORD LIST
- congruent
- figure
- corresponding
- segment
- angle
- polygons
- regular
- diagonal
- rhombus
- vertex
- hypotenuse

Across:
5. Matching
6. Corner
9. Side of a triangle opposite a 90 degree angle
10. Figures with straight lines
11. Part or section

Down:
1. Point of intersection of 2 sides of an angle
2. Corresponding
3. Shape
4. Slanting
7. Quadrilateral with opposite sides equal and parallel
8. All sides and angles equal

Let's Read these "shapely" books.
101 Science Surprises by Roy Richards
The Boy with Square Eyes by Juliet Snape and Charles Snape

Extension Keep a geometric journal. For 1 week, keep track of the number of various geometric shapes you encounter. For example, in how many ways do you see circles represented? Try to give examples of geometric shapes found in nature. Look around your house. Look around the school. Look around malls. Your list could be quite long!

© Steck-Vaughn Company   87   Spelling 6, SV 6717-6

Name_____ Date _____

Math
Geometry p. 3

WORD LIST
- congruent
- figure
- corresponding
- segment
- angle
- polygons
- regular
- diagonal
- rhombus
- vertex
- hypotenuse

Label the pictures with words from the Word List. If a picture can be identified with more than 1 of the words from the Word List, you will see 2 lines. One word is not used to label the pictures. Use that word in a sentence that relates to geometry.

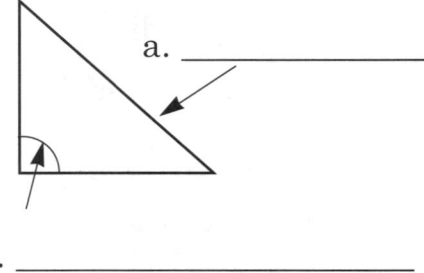

a. _____

b. _____

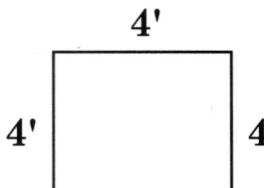

f. _____

c. _____

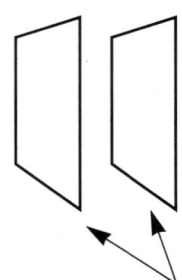

g. _____

h. _____

d. _____

e. _____

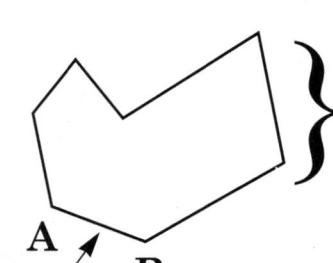

i. _____

j. _____

Name_____ Date _____

Math
Money p. 1

Write these words in alphabetical order on a separate sheet of paper. Remember, if more than one word begins with the same letter, look at the second, third, or maybe fourth letter in each word.

WORD LIST
- acccunt
- consumers
- percent
- annually
- received
- expenses
- discount
- prices
- decrease
- earnings
- allowance

1. Write the words that contain a double consonant.

   _____   _____
   _____

2. Write the words that are plural.

   _____   _____
   _____   _____

3. Write the words that contain the **ē** sound.

   _____   _____

4. Write the words that contain the **ow** sound.

   _____   _____
   _____

5. Write the words that end with the **t** sound.

   _____   _____
   _____

 **TRY THIS** Brainstorm and list the things on which you spend your allowance or other money you earn. List at least 3 other ways in which you can earn money. List ways in which you can save money. Share your ideas with the class. By sharing, you might get some good ideas from your classmates.

 **LET'S WRITE** Many of the words in the Word List are used when talking about money, shopping, or buying. Create a comic strip using 1 of the themes listed or a theme of your own. The comic strip should be at least 4 frames. Use at least 5 words from the Word List in the dialogue between characters in the comic strip. Share the comic strip with the class.

Name_____ Date_____

Math
Money p. 2

WORD LIST
- account
- consumers
- percent
- annually
- received
- expenses
- discount
- prices
- decrease
- earnings
- allowance

Write the word (or words) from the Word List that best fits each clue.

1. Salary or wages　　　　_____

2. Yearly　　　　_____

3. Money given weekly or monthly, often to a child　　　　_____

4. Costs of things　　　　_____

5. Reduction or cut　　　　_____
　　　　_____

6. Charges made within one's work　　　　_____

7. What % stands for　　　　_____

8. Shoppers or buyers　　　　_____

9. Acquired or obtained　　　　_____

10. An exact list of money given and received　　　　_____

Let's Read these "money-saving" books.
Not for a Billion Gazillion Dollars by Paula Danziger
Money to Burn by E.M. Goldman

Extension　　Research and make a chart about money in other countries, or what is known as "foreign currency." Indicate the country and what the currency is called, as well as its value compared to the American dollar. If possible, include when this money as it is known began. For example, in Mexico, *peso* is a term used. Try to find out its value in relationship to our dollar. Find out when the peso was first used. Try to research at least 5 countries. Share your findings with the class.

Math
Money p. 3

WORD LIST
- account
- consumers
- percent
- annually
- received
- expenses
- discount
- prices
- decrease
- earnings
- allowance

Complete the passage with words from the Word List.

The twins each ❶ _____ an ❷ _____ of $5.00 a week. In the summer, they did extra jobs, like cutting their neighbor's lawn, walking dogs for people, and baby-sitting. Their ❸ _____ during the summer months were three times as much as their allowances. The twins were told they had to save 5% (five ❹ _____) of what they earned, and that was okay with them. They were also told they had to pay for any extra ❺ _____, or costs, involved in their extra jobs. Of course, since the jobs were so close to home, the twins didn't have to worry about extra expenses. When it was time for school, the twins decided they wanted to help pay for some of the things they would need. They each made a list of things they wanted the most. Then, they checked the ❻ _____, or costs, of these things. They made sure to check to see which stores might have a markdown, or a ❼ _____, on certain things. Any ❽ _____ in price would help them save money. The twins proved to be smart ❾ _____, or shoppers. They saved quite a bit of money by comparing store prices. The twins were anxious to see their bank ❿ _____ continue to grow, so they didn't spend their money foolishly. When they saw what they had saved in just a few months, they knew that ⓫ _____ they could save qu a bit!

Name_____ Date_____

Math
Tools/Terms p. 1

WORD LIST
- compass
- protractor
- calculator
- matrix
- principal
- palindrome
- logic
- interest
- graph
- geometry
- formula

Write these words in alphabetical order on a separate sheet of paper. Remember, if more than one word begins with the same letter, look at the second, third, or maybe fourth letter in each word.

1. Write the words in the correct columns.

1-syllable word **2-syllable words**
_____ _____
                            _____
                            _____
                            _____

3-syllable words **4-syllable words**
_____ _____
_____ _____
_____
_____
_____

2. Write the word that ends with the **f** sound.

_____

3. Write the word that ends with the **k** sound.

_____

The Word List includes 11 tools and terms used in the field of mathematics. Can you think of other tools or terms that have not been listed on any of the Word Lists in this unit? For example, would you ever use a thermometer in math? Would you ever use a book? Brainstorm and list at least 10 other terms or tools that would be used in mathematics. Remember, there are some words that have a particular meaning just for math; for example, the word *interest*. When you are finished, share your words with the class. Make a master list of all new terms. Make sure you know the meanings or the uses for the tools or terms.

Name_____ Date _____

Math
Tools/Terms p. 2

Complete the puzzle with words from the Word List.

Across:
1. Principles of reasoning
5. Drawing showing relationship between sets of numbers
6. Number which reads the same forward and backward
9. Used to measure angles

WORD LIST
- compass
- protractor
- calculator
- matrix
- principal
- palindrome
- logic
- interest
- graph
- geometry
- formula

Down:
2. Tool for doing math quickly
3. Set of symbols for a math rule
4. Amount charged for a loan
5. Study of space and figures
6. Amount loaned to someone
7. Table
8. Used to draw circles

 Design a catalog for math. The catalog may contain tools as well as games and books that might help to make math fun or to teach math. Use at least 4 words from the Word List in your catalog. In a catalog, for each item identified, you should describe each game or tool. Try to have include least 10 items. Don't forget to create a catalog cover. Display the catalogs around the room.

 Let's Read and have fun with these books.
Summer Business by Charles E. Martin
Test Your Math IQ by Steve Ryan

Name_____ Date_____

Math
Tools/Terms p. 3

WORD LIST
- compass
- protractor
- calculator
- matrix
- principal
- palindrome
- logic
- interest
- graph
- geometry
- formula

Label the following with words from the Word List.

_____ (compass)

242 _____

_____ (calculator)

_____ (graph)

(area = l x w) _____

_____ (protractor)

_____ (shapes)

_____ (matrix/table)

Complete the passages with words from the Word List.

1. The _____ is the amount of a debt

    Minus the _____ which will be charged, you can bet!

2. You follow a recipe to bake a cake or cook fish.

    You use a _____ to figure the circumference of a dish.

Make up some other rhymes using other words from the Word List. Be sure to use the word *logic* in 1 of your rhymes.

Extension Create a story telling the "why" of something in math. The story may be humorous and/or it may contain some facts. Some suggestions for story titles include: Why a Zero? Why Money? Why Numbers? When you have finished the story, have a partner proofread it before you do a final version. Publish the final versions in one book entitled "Whys of Math!" Share the book with others and display in the school library.

SPELLING GRADE 6
Answer Key

P. 5 1. industry, efficient, inventions 2. 2-syllable: textiles, labor, products, machines, wages 3-syllable: factories, industry, efficient, inventions 4-syllable: revolution, transportation 3. factories

P. 6 1. wages 2. labor 3. efficient 4. transportation 5. factories 6. textiles 7. products 8. industry 9. machines 10. revolution 11. inventions; Steam-Powered Locomotive

P. 7 1. inventions 2. factories 3. machines 4. products 5. efficient 6. revolution 7. industry 8. labor 9. wages

P. 8 1. deserts, temperatures, dunes 2. precipitation, formation 3. arctic, Antarctic, harsh 4. equator, evaporate 5. deserts, arctic, adapt

P. 9 ACROSS: 1. Antarctic 2. precipitation 5. dunes 8. evaporate 9. deserts 10. formation DOWN: 1. adapt 3. equator 4. temperatures 5. arctic 6. harsh

P. 10 1. deserts 2. precipitation 3. evaporate 4. temperatures 5. harsh 6. adapt 7. dunes 8. formation

P. 11 1. issues, speech, support 2. party, integrity 3. politics, candidate, election 4. speech, vote 5. campaign 6. issues, leaders

P. 12 ACROSS: 2. election 3. candidate 5. speech 6. party 7. issues 9. politics 10. integrity DOWN: 1. vote 3. campaign 4. leaders 8. support

P. 13 1. politics 2. election 3. vote 4. candidate 5. campaign 6. issues 7. leaders 8. party 9. support 10. speech 11. integrity

P. 14 1. artifacts, ruins, temples, monuments 2. society, archaeology 3. civilization, flourish, vanished 4. flourish, ancient, explore, ruins, vanished, temples

P. 15 1. ancient 2. ruins or artifacts, archaeology 3. vanished 4. flourish 5. explore 6. civilization ACROSS: 1. artifacts 3. monuments DOWN: 2. temples 4. society

P. 16 1. civilization 2. society 3. archaeology 4. artifacts 5. ancient 6. ruins 7. vanished 8. flourish 9. temples 10. monuments 11. explore

P. 17 1. toils, dangers, immigrants 2. establish, immigrants, potential 3. dangers, comfort, risking, voyage, embark, depart 4. opportunity

P. 18 1. toils 2. depart 3. voyage 4. opportunity 5. potential 6. embark 7. dangers 8. immigrants 9. comfort 10. establish 11. risking

P. 19 1. immigrants 2. establish 3. comfort 4. embark 5. depart 6. voyage 7. risking 8. opportunity 9. dangers 10. toils 11. potential

P. 20 1. sombrero, poncho, cocoa, fiesta, adobe, piñata 2. neighbor, border, exports 3. neighbor, maize 4. lariat, fiesta, piñata

P. 21 ACROSS: 1. cocoa 6. sombrero 7. border 8. exports 10. neighbor 11. maize DOWN: 2. adobe 3. poncho 4. lariat 5. fiesta 9. piñata

P. 22 1. neighbor 2. border 3. adobe 4. fiesta 5. exports

P. 23 1. 2-syllable: vivid, texture, marvels, critics, image, vibrant, tragic, depressed 3-syllable: distinctive, influence 2. image, tragic 3. style

P. 24 1. vibrant, vivid 2. distinctive 3. tragic, depressed 4. texture ACROSS: 1. influence 3. marvels DOWN: 1. image 2. critics 3. style

P. 25 1. distinctive 2. style 3. marvels 4. image 5. influence 6. vivid 7. vibrant 8. texture 9. depressed 10. critics 11. tragic

P. 26 1. designed, complemented, inspired, harmonized 2. materials, traditions 3. spacious 4. modern, natural 5. designed, architect 6. landscape

P. 27 1. architect 2. spacious 3. modern 4. natural 5. inspired ACROSS: 2. complemented 4. landscape 6. harmonized DOWN: 1. designed 3. materials 5. traditions

P. 28 1. architect 2. designed 3. inspired 4. complemented 5. natural 6. landscape 7. materials 8. spacious 9. modern 10. harmonized 11. traditions

P. 29 1. 2-syllable: disease, viral, vaccine 3-syllable: infectious, contagious, transmitted, injection, prescription 4-syllable: epidemic, bacterial 5-syllable: antibiotics 2. transmitted, vaccine 3. prescription, injection 4. infectious, contagious

P. 30 1. viral 2. disease 3. transmitted 4. bacterial 5. infectious or contagious 6. epidemic 7. prescription 8. injection 9. contagious or infectious 10. antibiotics 11. vaccine

P. 31 1. infectious 2. disease 3. transmitted 4. contagious 5. epidemic 6. bacterial 7. antibiotics 8. prescription 9. injection 10. viral 11. vaccine

P. 32 1. boundaries, singles, doubles, points 2. tennis, opponent 3. racquet, match 4. deuce, court, points, match 5. server

P. 33 ACROSS: 3. boundaries 6. singles 8. server 9. court 11. match DOWN: 1. doubles 2. tennis 4. racquet 5. points 7. deuce 10. opponent

P. 34 1. tennis 2. singes 3. doubles 4. match 5. server 6. opponent 7. points 8. deuce

P. 35 1. cultures, guitarists, costumes, horns 2. strolling, blending 3. accordion, emotion 4. mariachi, ranchero 5. folk, guitarists

P. 36 ACROSS: 3. costumes 5. mariachi 9. ranchero 10. cultures 11. guitarists DOWN: 1. accordion 2. emotion 4. strolling 6. horns 7. blending 8. folk

P. 37 1. folk 2. emotion 3. mariachi 4. costumes 5. strolling 6. ranchero

P. 38 1. 1-syllable: beats 2-syllable: patterns, verses, chorus, rhythm 3-syllable: accented, crescendo 4-syllable: repetition, variation, original, syncopation 2. patterns, beats, verses 3. patterns, accented 4. crescendo

P. 39 1. repetition, variation 2. verses, chorus 3. accented, beats 4. original 5. syncopation 6. crescendo 7. patterns 8. rhythm

P. 40 1. chorus, verses 2. patterns, repetition, original, variation 3. beats, rhythm, accented, syncopation 4. crescendo

P. 41 1. stopwatch 2. funnel, goggles, mirrors 3. beakers, mirrors, corks, slides 4. magnet 5. thermometer 6. microscope, scale

P. 42 1. microscope 2. thermometer, scale 3. goggles 4. beakers 5. corks 6. mirrors, stopwatch 7. magnet 8. slides 9. funnel

P. 44 1. appendix, swallow, dissolve 2. tongue, stomach 3. 1-syllable: tongue, mouth 2-syllable: stomach, liver, swallow, dissolve 3-syllable: intestine, appendix, digestion, saliva 4. esophagus

P. 45 ACROSS: 2. esophagus 4. stomach 5. liver 7. mouth 9. intestine 10. saliva 11. appendix DOWN: 1. dissolve 3. swallow 6. digestion 8. tongue

P. 46 1. digestion 2. saliva 3. dissolve 4. swallow

P. 47 1. on-line, download, bookmark 2. Internet, navigate, cyberspace, virtual 3. navigate, communicate, cyberspace 4. bookmarks, sources 5. browser, download 6. research

P. 48 1. browser 2. download 3. Internet 4. navigate 5. bookmarks 6. cyberspace 7. research 8. communicate 9. on-line 10. virtual 11. sources; Information Superhighway

P. 49 1. on-line 2. communicate 3. browser 4. download 5. navigate 6. bookmarks 7. research 8. sources

P. 50 1. changes, atoms, elements, compounds, experiments, reactions 2. matter, surrounded 3. atoms, elements, experiments, energy 4. nucleus, structure, compounds, reactions

P. 51 ACROSS: 1. compounds 4. atoms 7. reactions 8. energy 10. elements DOWN: 1. changes 2. nucleus 3. surrounded 5. matter 6. structure 8. experiments

P. 52 1. matter 2. elements 3. atoms 4. compounds 5. structure 6. nucleus 7. surrounded 8. reactions 9. changes 10. energy 11. experiments

P. 53 1. traits, chromosomes, cells, genes 2. 1-syllable: traits, cells, genes 2-syllable: offspring, cloning, membrane 3-syllable: chromosomes, inherit, dominant, recessive 4-syllable: generation

P. 54 1. membrane 2. chromosomes 3. cells 4. traits 5. cloning 6. dominant 7. genes 8. generation 9. inherit 10. offspring 11. recessive, Gregor Mendel

P. 55 1. inherit 2. traits 3. cloning 4. offspring 5. genes 6. dominant 7. recessive 8. generation

P. 56 1. satellite, constellation 2. galaxy, asteroid, atmosphere, meteor, telescope, satellite, universe, gravity 3. sunspot, nova

P. 57 1. asteroid 2. atmosphere 3. gravity 4. meteor 5. satellite 6. nova 7. sunspot 8. telescope 9. galaxy 10. constellation 11. universe, Capricorn

P. 58 1. universe 2. galaxy 3. gravity 4. atmosphere

P. 59 1. 1-syllable: spear 2-syllable: spasm, panic, shelter, threaten, frightened 3-syllable: turbulence, survival, incessant, frustration 5-syllable: infuriating 2. threaten, frightened, frustration, infuriating, turbulence, survival

P. 60 ACROSS: 2. frustration 4. panic 6. shelter 8. spasm 9. infuriating 10. spear DOWN: 1. turbulence 3. incessant 5. frightened 7. survival 9. threaten

P. 61 1. threaten 2. frustration 3. spasm 4. survival 5. panic 6. shelter 7. spear 8. turbulence 9 frightened 10. infuriating 11. incessant

P. 62 1. narrative, descriptive 2. emphasize, summarize 3. chronological, importance 4. accurate, arrange, summarize, narrative 5. contrast, details, arrange 6. comparison

P. 63 1. chronological 2. summarize 3. comparison 4. accurate 5. arrange 6. importance 7. narrative 8. emphasize 9. details 10. descriptive 11. contrast

P. 64 1. details 2. descriptive 3. narrative 4. arrange 5. chronological 6. importance 7. comparison 8. contrast 9. accurate 10. emphasize 11. summarize

P. 65 1. mythology, poetry, imagery, biography 2. mythology 3. belief, vivid 4. imagination, adaptation 5. biography, significant, belief, phenomenon 6. prose

P. 66 1. vivid 2. belief 3. significant 4. imagery 5. poetry, prose ACROSS: 2. mythology 4. adaptation 5. phenomenon DOWN: 1. imagination 3. biography

P. 67 1. a. imagination b. vivid c. mythology d. belief e. phenomenon f. adaptation 2. a. biography b. significant c. prose d. poetry e. imagery

P. 68 1. mechanics, experts, periodicals 2. thesis, statement, outline, revise, grammar, credit, experts 3. documentation/document, periodicals/period 4. clarity

P. 69 1. experts 2. clarity 3. documentation 4. periodicals 5. credit 6. thesis 7. outline 8. grammar 9. mechanics 10. revise 11. statement

P. 70 1. experts 2. credit 3. documentation 4. thesis 5. statement 6. clarity 7. revise 8. mechanics 9. grammar

P. 71 1. experiences, observations, memories 2. daily, diary 3. personal, dialogue, reflection, memories, diary 4. log 5. respond, travel, daily

P. 72 1. personal 2. dialogue 3. daily 4. respond 5. experiences, memories ACROSS: 2. observations 4. diary 5. log DOWN: 1. reflection 3. travel

P. 73 1. experiences 2. memories 3. daily 4. personal 5. diary 6. respond 7. dialogue 8. observations 9. reflection

P. 74 1. stereotype, circulation, advertising, propaganda 2. libel, format, anchor, bias 3. commercial, media 4. slant 5. anchor

P. 75 1. anchor 2. media 3. format 4. slant 5. circulation 6. advertising 7. libel 8. bias 9. propaganda 10. commercial 11. stereotype

P. 76 1. media 2. format 3. anchor 4. commercial 5. advertising 6. circulation 7. slant 8. propaganda 9. bias 10. stereotype 11. libel

P. 77 1. mean, median, frequency 2. outcomes, diagrams 3. range, favorable 4. probability 5. mean, mode, range, chance 6. surveyed

P. 78 1. favorable 2. chance 3. probability 4. mean 5. mode 6. median 7. frequency 8. diagrams 9. surveyed 10. outcomes 11. range

P. 79 1. frequency, outcomes, diagrams 2. probability, surveyed, favorable, chance, mean, median, mode, range

P. 80 1. plane, data 2. quadrants, coordinates, axes 3. horizontal, coordinates 4. vertical, collecting, prediction, reporting, origin

P. 81 ACROSS: 2. plane 4. coordinates 6. vertical 9. prediction 11. collecting DOWN: 1. horizontal 3. axes 5. quadrants 7. data 8. reporting 10. origin

P. 82 1. quadrants 2. vertical 3. horizontal 4. axes 5. origin 6. coordinates 7. reporting 8. data 9. collecting 10. prediction

P. 83 1. associative, commutative 2. 1-syllable: base 2-syllable: factors 3-syllable: expression, exponent, calculate, expanded 4-syllable: binomial, coefficient, operations, commutative 3. expression, coefficient, associative, commutative

P. 84 1. factors 2. expression 3. coefficient 4. commutative 5. associative 6. exponent 7. expanded 8. binomial 9. base 10. operations 11. calculate

P. 85 a. exponent b. base c. commutative d. coefficient e. associative f. binomial g. factors h. expanded 1. operations 2. calculate 3. expression

P. 86 1. 2-syllable: figure, segment, angle, rhombus, vertex 3-syllable: congruent, polygons, regular 4-syllable: corresponding, diagonal, hypotenuse 2. rhombus

P. 87 ACROSS: 5. corresponding 6. angle 9. hypotenuse 10. polygons 11. segment DOWN: 1. vertex 2. congruent 3. figure 4. diagonal 7. rhombus 8. regular

P. 88 a. hypotenuse b. angle c. rhombus d. diagonal e. vertex f. regular g. congruent h. polygons i. figure j. segment

P. 89 1. account, annually, allowance 2. consumers, expenses, prices, earnings 3. received, decrease 4. account, discount, allowance 5. account, percent, discount

P. 90 1. earnings 2. annually 3. allowance 4. prices 5. discount, decrease 6. expenses 7. percent 8. consumers 9. received 10. account

P. 91 1. received 2. allowance 3. earnings 4. percent 5. expenses 6. prices 7. discount 8. decrease 9. consumers 10. account 11. annually

P. 92 1. 1-syllable: graph 2-syllable: compass, matrix, logic 3-syllable: protractor, principal, palindrome, interest, formula 4-syllable: calculator, geometry 2. graph 3. logic

P. 93 ACROSS: 1. logic 5. graph 6. palindrome 9. protractor DOWN: 2. calculator 3. formula 4. interest 5. geometry 6. principal 7. matrix 8. compass

P. 94 1. principal, interest 2. formula